Selected and edited by Abi May
Cover design: Gentian Suçi
Design: M-A Mignot based on a design
    by Gentian Suçi
ISBN: 978-3-03730-704-5

© Aurora Production AG, Switzerland, 2012
Printed in Taiwan.

www.auroraproduction.com

quiet moments
FOR BUSY DAYS

Selections by Abi May

ACKNOWLEDGEMENTS

Quiet Moments collections have been derived largely from *Activated*, an international magazine published since 1995, edited by Keith Phillips. Alex Peterson is an *Activated* staff writer, and Abi May is a frequent contributor.

Quotations attributed to Jesus but not followed by Bible references are excerpts of personal messages that individuals received from Jesus while in prayer.

Aurora Production AG would like to thank all those who submitted their writings and prayers for publication; copyright holders have been identified where possible and we apologize for any inadvertent omissions.

CONTENTS

Foreword

Do you ever feel as though you are an athlete competing in a long-distance race? You can't stop or you'll be overtaken by the demands of life. But unlike running a marathon, in the race of life you need to take a break sometimes—energy expended must be recouped. Pausing during busy days can take a determined effort, but it is well worth it. Having a snack or a drink, taking a short nap, or having a quick shower can refresh you, but these practical measures don't go far enough. Your mind and spirit need refreshment too.

That's where *Quiet Moments for Busy Days* comes in. Even pausing for five minutes to read a page or two can provide a spiritual lift. If you can take a few minutes longer, read a chapter. Maybe it's your coffee break, maybe it's over lunch, maybe it's in that little pause before you go to pick up the children from school, maybe it's in the moments before you start cooking a meal. Take a deep breath, take a deep spiritual breath, "be transformed by the renewing of your mind,"[1] and once renewed, you'll be ready to keep on running.

Abi May
August 2011

[1] Romans 12:2

1

Who Am I?

ARE NOT FIVE SPARROWS SOLD FOR TWO COPPER COINS? AND NOT
ONE OF THEM IS FORGOTTEN BEFORE GOD. BUT THE VERY HAIRS
OF YOUR HEAD ARE ALL NUMBERED. DO NOT FEAR THEREFORE;
YOU ARE OF MORE VALUE THAN MANY SPARROWS.

Luke 12:6–7

Each person is a V.S.P. (Very Special Person) because
we are each created in the image of God.
Desmond Tutu

Friendship with oneself is all important, because without it
one cannot be friends with anyone else in the world.
Eleanor Roosevelt

If God had wanted me otherwise,
He would have created me otherwise.
Johann Wolfgang von Goethe

Do not wish to be anything but what you are,
and try to be that perfectly.
Francis de Sales

Each of us is unique in God's eyes. Each of us is an individual,
and He wants us to express our individuality. He's not trying
to press us all into one mold, so that we all look the same and
act the same, and do things exactly the same way.
Maria Fontaine ■

The cracked pot

WE CARRY THIS PRECIOUS MESSAGE AROUND IN THE UNADORNED
CLAY POTS OF OUR ORDINARY LIVES. THAT'S
TO PREVENT ANYONE FROM CONFUSING GOD'S
INCOMPARABLE POWER WITH US.
2 Corinthians 4:7 (THE MESSAGE)

Long ago, a water bearer in India had two large pots. Each hung on one end of a pole, which he carried across his shoulders. One of the pots had a crack in it. The other pot was perfect and always delivered a full portion of water at the end of the long walk from the stream to the master's house, but the cracked pot arrived only half full.

For a full two years this went on daily, with the bearer delivering only one and a half pots full of water to his master's house after each trip to the stream. Of course, the perfect pot was proud of its accomplishments, perfect to the end for which it was made. But the poor cracked pot was ashamed of its own imperfection and miserable that it was able to accomplish only half of what it had been made to do. Perceiving itself to be a bitter failure, the cracked pot spoke to the water bearer one day by the stream.

"I am ashamed of myself, and I want to apologize to you."

"Why?" asked the bearer. "What are you ashamed of?"

"I have been able, for these past two years, to deliver only half my load because this crack in my side causes water to leak out all the way back to your master's house. Because of my flaws, you have to do all of this work, and you don't get full value from your efforts," the pot said.

The water bearer felt sorry for the old cracked pot, and in his compassion he said, "As we return to the master's house, I want you to notice the flowers along the path."

Indeed, as they went up the hill, the old cracked pot took notice of the beautiful flowers beside the path, and this cheered it some. But at the end of the trail, it still felt bad because it had again leaked half its load, and so again it apologized to the bearer for its failure.

But the bearer said to the pot, "Did you notice that there were flowers only on your side of the path? That's because I have always known about your flaw, and I took advantage of it. I planted flower seeds on your side of the path, and every day while we walk back from the stream, you've watered them.

"For two years I have been able to pick these beautiful flowers to decorate my master's table. Without you being just the way you are, he would not have this beauty to grace his house."

Each of us has our own unique "flaws." We're all cracked pots. But if we will allow it, Jesus will use our flaws to grace His Father's table. As God calls you to the tasks He has appointed for you, don't be afraid of your flaws. Acknowledge them, and allow Him to take advantage of them, and you, too, can be the cause of beauty along His pathway.

Author unknown ■

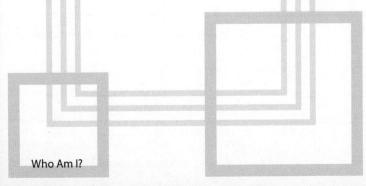

You're special!

You are part of a magnificent, vast, overall plan. You can't see that plan, but I can. You can't see how beautifully you fit in with the overall panorama of life and the balance of the universe, but I can. Someday you will see it too, and you will marvel together with Me at how wonderfully it all came together and how perfect it all is.

You are unique. There has never been a person like you, nor will there ever be another just like you. That's one of the things I like most about you. Resist the temptation to look negatively at yourself and focus on what you think are your shortcomings. What you perceive as imperfections, I perceive as uniqueness. What is perfection, after all? It is fulfilling the purpose for which you were created, which is to love and be loved. I love you just the way you are, and I love you as though you were the only person in the world.

A message from Jesus received in prayer ∎

> HE SAID TO ME, "MY GRACE IS SUFFICIENT FOR YOU, FOR MY
> STRENGTH IS MADE PERFECT IN WEAKNESS."
> *2 Corinthians 12:9*

To one degree or another, just about all of us are unsatisfied with ourselves—but that's not necessarily a bad thing. A certain amount of dissatisfaction is necessary if we're going to keep making progress. To become all that we can be, we must dream of being more than we are. The problem is that too many of us stop there, in the dream stage. Why do you suppose that is?

I suspect that more often than not it's because we don't think we have what it takes to turn our dreams into reality. And we're usually right about that. We can make some changes by sheer willpower or working harder, like reaching a new sales quota or dropping a dress or pants size. But what about the bigger changes, the changes inside that we know would make us happier and better people? It's that kind of change that is often most elusive.

We're not good enough, we tell ourselves. We have too many flaws and make too many mistakes. We've tried and failed too many times. What's the use? It's just not in us! Jesus summed it up simply when He said, "With men it is impossible, but not with God; for with God all things are possible."[1] The secret lies in putting ourselves in God's hands and letting Him do the impossible for us and through us and sometimes in spite of us. We may be small and weak and incapable, but there is a very big, strong, capable God just waiting to give us a hand. With His help, it's easier than you ever imagined to make those "impossible" changes in yourself.

Keith Phillips ∎

[1] Mark 10:27

The first step in learning to swim
is learning to float, and that starts
with learning to relax and not fight
the water. Put yourself in God's
hands, lie back, relax, and let
Him support you. Practice in the
shallows, and you will be ready for
whatever the future may hold.
Keith Phillips

Reflect upon your blessings,
of which every man has plenty,
not on your past misfortunes,
of which all men have some.
Charles Dickens

I HAVE LEARNED IN WHATEVER STATE I AM, TO BE CONTENT:
I KNOW HOW TO BE ABASED, AND I KNOW HOW TO ABOUND.
Philippians 4:11–12

Twenty-five years ago I came across a gem of wisdom that was to save my sanity. The thing that amazes me now is how easily I could have missed it. I was feeling happy and fulfilled at the time, satisfied with my life and where it seemed to be taking me. I could have brushed it aside as not applying to me, but I was soon glad I hadn't. Things took an unexpected downward turn, I lost my job and the security it had provided, and those words became a reference point that helped me get through the next few difficult months.

"If we would find our security in the knowledge that God loves us and has a plan for our lives, instead of relying on other things to meet that need, He could make us very happy. But we sometimes make ourselves unhappy by being dissatisfied, because we haven't learned, as the apostle Paul did, to be content in whatever state we're in."

That doesn't mean we should stop striving to be better people. We also shouldn't adopt a fatalist attitude when our circumstances aren't what they could or should be.

But getting back to my experience of 25 years ago, that little bit of advice helped me realize that while my circumstances had suddenly changed, that didn't change the things that counted most in life. It didn't change who I was or my main goals, nor did it change God's love for me. Therefore it shouldn't rob me of the contentment I'd had before things fell apart. The happy ending? By focusing on what I still had and not what I had lost, I made it through that difficult time and came out happier in the end.

Keith Phillips ∎

CHAPTER 2

The Pause Button

A PERSIAN FABLE SAYS, ONE DAY
A WANDERER FOUND A PIECE OF CLAY
SO REDOLENT OF SWEET PERFUME,
ITS ODOR SCENTED ALL THE ROOM.
"WHAT ARE THOU?" WAS THE QUICK DEMAND.
"ART THOU SOME GEM OF SAMARKAND,
OR SPIKENARD RARE IN ODD DISGUISE?
OR OTHER COSTLY MERCHANDISE?"
"NAY, I AM BUT A PIECE OF CLAY."
"THEN, WHENCE THIS WONDROUS SWEETNESS, PRAY?"
"FRIEND, IF THE SECRET I DISCLOSE,
I HAVE BEEN LIVING WITH THE ROSE."

Author unknown

Christians are supposed to try to be like Jesus—living as He would, acting as He would, speaking as He would, and even thinking as He would. But how do we accomplish that? How can we be more like Him? As in the Persian fable, it comes from living close to Jesus.

Many of us do spend time with Jesus, but how much quality time do we spend with Him, where we shut out the business of the day and give Him our full attention, communing with Him, enjoying Him, and getting to know Him better in order to become more like Him? If we don't, no matter how many good qualities we possess or how dynamic we are or how dedicated we are, no matter how good we are with people or what else we may have going for us, if we're not spending time with Jesus, we're not going to be a very good reflection of Him or His love to others.

The dictionary defines "communion" as "a feeling of emotional or spiritual closeness, a connection." So communing with Jesus means to make an emotional and spiritual connection with Jesus. Praise, prayer, and reading God's Word are all ways of making and sustaining that connection. These are the lifeblood of our spiritual lives.

Peter Amsterdam ■

Take a load off

COME TO ME, ALL YOU WHO LABOR AND ARE HEAVY LADEN, AND I
WILL GIVE YOU REST. TAKE MY YOKE UPON YOU AND LEARN FROM
ME, FOR I AM GENTLE AND LOWLY IN HEART,
AND YOU WILL FIND REST FOR YOUR SOULS. FOR MY YOKE
IS EASY AND MY BURDEN IS LIGHT.

Matthew 11:28–30

I have a riddle for you. What could seem to make a little more work
now, but save much more work in the long run?

Here are some hints. It is mentioned repeatedly in the Bible, and
those who have accomplished the most for God have all depended on
it. It is a life-altering concept, but also one that is often hard to grasp
because it goes contrary to natural reasoning.

The answer is "resting in Jesus." That means stopping what we're
doing and taking a little time to get quiet and plug in to Jesus in
spirit in order to be renewed and regenerated. Then we need to learn
to take that restful spirit with us as we go back to whatever we were
doing, so circumstances won't weigh so heavily on us and eventually
wear us out.

It sounds simple enough, but it's not always easy to do, especially at first. One big reason is that it goes against our natural bent. When we have so much to do, the last thing we feel like doing is slowing down, taking time to pray and read God's Word, and letting Him speak to us. That's not what we feel like doing or what seems sensible when we have a deadline or life is speeding along all around us.

But if we look at the lives of those who have done great things for God, we find many examples of people who relied on this principle. In fact, Jesus Himself needed such times of resting and refilling, according to several accounts in the Gospels. One says that having risen long before daylight, He went to a solitary place to pray.[1] Another says that He continued all night in prayer to God,[2] and another that it was His custom to go to the Mount of Olives to pray.[3]

We can't learn to rest in the Lord if we're not doing our part by pulling away from the fray. If we've been busy, busy, busy, then when our spirits need a rest we are usually swamped with thoughts about all there still is to do.

But if we can get in the habit of stopping our work long enough to turn our concerns over to Jesus and draw new strength and inspiration from Him, we won't be so tied into the vicious cycle of pushing ourselves beyond our limits and falling further behind. Instead, we will create a positive cycle where He strengthens us for the tasks at hand, and as a result we will have more faith to place our burdens on His shoulders and trust Him to take care of things.

Resting in Jesus means not trying to bear the burdens ourselves. It means continually putting them back on Jesus' shoulders. It means doing our part in prayer, so He can do the heavy lifting. It means valuing our time with God enough to make time for it, and because of that, having more of His blessings and Spirit in everything we do, because we've given the weight to Jesus through prayer, rather than trying to carry it ourselves.

It's easy to get on our own little "treadmill" and feel that we have to keep running to keep up, and yet feel like we're not really getting anywhere. We need to have enough sense, before we get to that point, to step off and ask Jesus to help us get in step with Him again.

Maria Fontaine ■

¹ Mark 1:35

² Luke 6:12

³ Luke 22:39,41

The daily pause
A SPIRITUAL EXERCISE

BLESSED IS THE MAN WHO LISTENS TO ME,
WATCHING DAILY AT MY GATES,
WAITING AT THE POSTS OF MY DOORS.
Proverbs 8:34

Sometimes we get so busy rushing through life that we fail to take time to reflect and get in touch and in tune with our Maker. As a result, we can miss the point of it all. Life is about the journey, what we learn and experience along the way. The journey is also where we find Jesus and learn about Him.

Make the most of your journey this year by making a resolution to spend at least 10 or 15 minutes daily in prayer and reflection, alone with Jesus. Try to establish a regular time each day. Find what works best for you. Some people like to take their quiet time first thing, while others find it helpful to step back from their work at midday for spiritual refreshing, and others find it easiest in the evening.

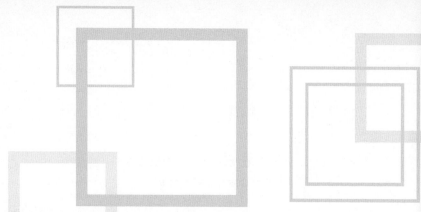

Vary the activities you use to fill this time. You may want to keep a little diary of what you do, writing down the different spiritual activities and lessons you learn. Here are some ideas to get you started.

Meditate on God's Word: Read a passage of Scripture or some other inspired material, then pause and think about how it applies to you.

Praise: Thank Jesus for His goodness and the blessings He bestows on you and those dear to you. Be specific.

Connect: Make a heart-to-heart connection with Jesus; receive His love and give Him yours.

Listen: Get quiet and see what Jesus has to say to you personally at that moment.

Pray: Ask Jesus to intercede and change situations for the better.[1] Pray for yourself, your loved ones, others whom you know are in need, world situations, etc.

Abi May ∎

[1] Romans 8:34; John 16:23

Refuge of meditation

I once visited a monastery that was built on the ruins of an ancient Roman fortress, set high atop a rocky crag in a Syrian desert. So steep was a series of 300 steps near the summit that supplies had to be hoisted the rest of the way using a cable system. Three stone archways at the top announced to my fellow pilgrims and me that we were nearing a sanctuary. Finally we had to squeeze through a small opening, no larger than two feet square, cut in the rock. Just then a jet passed so high overhead that it was recognizable only by the vapor trail it left in the azure sky—a silent, fitting reminder of how far we were removed from the rush and noise of the world we had left behind.

The monastery welcomes anyone seeking spiritual solace. My party of about 30 represented several faiths and perhaps a dozen nationalities. There is no charge for meals or lodging, only a request that visitors lend a hand with the chores and respect others' times of meditation.

Inside we were welcomed with a glass of tea and invited to sit and chat and enjoy the view. As we got to know one another, a sense of brotherhood instantly developed, despite our diverse backgrounds.

Sitting at a table, I talked with one of the monastery's volunteers who was French. He was in his early twenties, and I was curious to find out what motivated him to stay at this remote outpost so far from civilization.

"I have been here for two years now," he said in his charming accent. "I was a successful chief accountant for a prominent firm in France, with all the perks of a high-salaried job."

"So what was it that made you give all that up?" I asked.

"I felt unfulfilled. One day as I was sitting in a chapel, I had a vision that caused me to realize I had my priorities wrong. I needed to live in service for others. That's why I'm here."

That evening we were invited to celebrate Mass together underneath the painted fragments of a scene of heaven and hell, saints and sinners, followed by a simple meal and a time of solitary meditation.

The next day as I made my way back down to the valley, I gazed at the surrounding hills, stretching into the distance. The scenery spoke to me more than it had on the way up, when my mind was still full of going, doing, achieving.

I imagined water flowing through the dry riverbeds and cascading over precipices in thunderous glory. If rain came, it would truly be a wonder. It hadn't rained in four years.

The terrain appeared devoid of life, but upon closer examination all kinds of life could be seen on those steep slopes—lichen, exquisite minute wildflowers, and the occasional desert dweller, all struggling to survive. Even when our lives seem as dry and barren as those hills, with not much happening on the surface, God is busy at work.

As I reached the bottom of the hill, I determined to take a few minutes each day to make a temple of my heart.

Curtis Peter van Gorder ■

CHAPTER 3

My Circle

FRIENDS COME AND FRIENDS GO,

BUT A TRUE FRIEND STICKS BY YOU LIKE FAMILY.

Proverbs 18:24 (THE MESSAGE)

The course of true love never did run smooth.
William Shakespeare

Love is an act of endless forgiveness,
a tender look which becomes a habit.
Peter Ustinov

It's not love that blinds, but self-love.
Voltaire

Love is not getting, but giving. Love is … the best thing in
the world, and the thing that lives the longest.
Henry van Dyke

The heart of him who truly loves is a paradise on earth;
he has God in himself, for God is love.
Abbé Hugo Félicité de Lamennais ∎

All I have seen teaches
me to trust the
Creator for all
I have not seen.
Ralph Waldo Emerson

One word frees us
of all the weight and
pain of life: That
word is "love."
Sophocles

A perfect world

It was just a little thing, that smile on my baby's face, but it changed my perspective on life.

As he woke and looked up at me, he was looking at what mattered most in the world to him—me! He didn't care that his diaper needed changing or that I was dressed in mismatched pajamas, my hair a mess. He just loved me and loved being with me. He didn't need perfection; love made it all right. That moment of holding him and taking in those rays of love clarified something I'd been thinking about earlier.

The lack of perfection in life has always rubbed me the wrong way. When someone said or did something that irked me, I'd often argue my case against it in my mind. Perfection, I reasoned, was the only thing that could ever relieve my irritations. But I also knew that could never be. This was real life. I needed another option.

The more I thought about it, the more I realized that what I really wanted was for the world to revolve around me—my wishes, my feelings, my preferences, my priorities. Something had to change, and this time it had to be me, regardless of the faults of others. But how? I'd tried before.

Then that morning, as I held my baby, a whisper of a thought came to me. Would you want your baby to be perfect right from the start?

After pondering that thought, I couldn't imagine something I'd want less. If he'd been able to walk and run the day he was born, I'd never get to see the look of thrill and accomplishment on his face when he took his first steps, and I'd also miss that special feeling of holding him in my arms, knowing that he was completely dependent on me. If he had been able to talk perfectly from the time he was born, I'd never experience the joy of hearing him speak his first word. If he knew everything that an adult knows, I'd never get to see him overcome with wonder at some new discovery and I'd never have the fulfillment of teaching him something new. So many things I'd miss. No, his imperfection makes him just perfect. I wouldn't have him any other way!

What is it then, I asked myself, that makes his imperfection different from the other imperfections around me?

And the answer came. It's love.

That was it! That was what I was lacking. That was what I needed more of in order to cope bravely and cheerfully when confronted by problems I wished didn't exist.

Think how much you'd miss if you and everyone around you were perfect from the start. You'd miss the unpredictability of life that adds the sense of surprise; the joy of forgiving and being forgiven; the strong, abiding bonds of friendship that are formed through adversity, and the positive character traits that are formed much the same way.

Adding negative thoughts to a negative situation, I realized, never brings positive results. I determined then and there to look for and find the positive opportunities and experiences that are hidden behind the mask of imperfection.

Every situation and person we encounter can make our lives a ride of joy and surprise, if we look beyond. Difficulties, losses, hurts, lacks—think of each as a clue in a treasure hunt, the door to a secret vault where you will find beautiful treasures from God. "Ask, and it will be given to you; seek, and you will find; knock, and it will be opened to you."[1]

Chalsey Dooley ∎

[1] Matthew 7:7

Finding perfection

I remember, as a very little girl, looking out across the field behind our home at what appeared to be the perfect tree. I could hardly contain my excitement as I ran to inspect it up close. But as I reached out to gather some perfect leaves from the perfect tree, I had one of my first big disappointments. On closer inspection, each leaf was marred somehow—a scrape, a brown splotch, an insect bite. There wasn't one that I could take home and hang in my room as a symbol of perfection.

Images may appear perfect from a distance, but as we look closer we see the imperfections. We watch strangers drive by in their shiny new cars and assume that they have perfect lives, not realizing that they may have problems worse than our own. We watch television and movies and see images of perfection, illusions that fade as the final credits roll. A scenic view may look perfect from a distance, but up close we see the mud and the litter. The world looks better without binoculars or microscopes.

We look for perfection—perfect people, perfect situations, perfect relationships, perfect happiness—but because none of us are perfect, we wind up discouraged or disillusioned. But God isn't looking for perfection—at least not our idea of perfection. Sure, we can all do better, but often what we perceive as flaws and foibles are actually His doing, part of our unique makeup, blessings in disguise. And are all problems all bad? Aren't they sometimes God's way of steering us to better things?

God doesn't expect us to be perfect. All He asks is that we try our best to love Him and others.[1] When we do that, we can feel secure in His love, and that changes our whole outlook. We feel better about ourselves, and that helps us to see the best in others and to make the most of our circumstances. Life isn't perfect, but that's okay. God knew better.

Joyce Suttin ■

[1] Matthew 22:37–39

The two banquets

THIS IS THE MESSAGE THAT YOU HEARD FROM THE BEGINNING,
THAT WE SHOULD LOVE ONE ANOTHER.

1 John 3:11

A person had a dream in which heaven and hell were pictured as two banquets.

In hell the tables stretched for as far as the eye could see, and they were all filled with every possible good thing to eat and drink. People were seated at the tables, but they were all starving, emaciated, skin-on-skeleton figures. A closer look revealed that they were chained in such a way that they could reach the food and pick it up, but the chains prevented them from bringing the food to their mouths. In the ultimate cruelty, they were dying of starvation with food in their hands.

In heaven the tables also stretched for as far as the eye could see, and they were filled with all the same wonderful choices as in hell. And just as in hell, the people were all chained in such a way that they could pick up the food but not bring it to their own mouths. However, in this banquet hall, the people were all healthy, laughing, singing, and enjoying themselves. The difference? In heaven they had realized that although they couldn't feed themselves, the chains allowed them to feed each other.

Author unknown ■

Pass on the praise

"You're a great wife, and I don't know what I would do without you." And as he spoke, he put his arms around her and kissed her, and she forgot all her cares in that moment.

And, forgetting it all, she sang as she washed the dishes, and she sang as she made the beds.

And the song was heard by the woman next door, and she caught the refrain and sang also.

And as the neighbor sang, a delivery boy who came to her door heard it and went away whistling the tune.

And the world heard the whistle.

And it was all because he had told her he loved her.

Author unknown ■

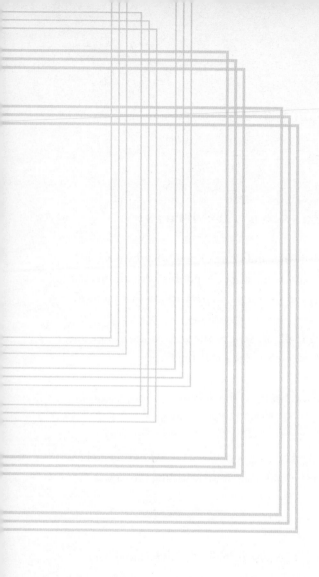

Quiet Moments for Busy Days

CHAPTER 4

The Miracle of Life

LIFT UP YOUR EYES ON HIGH,
AND SEE WHO HAS CREATED THESE THINGS,
WHO BRINGS OUT THEIR HOST BY NUMBER;
HE CALLS THEM ALL BY NAME,
BY THE GREATNESS OF HIS MIGHT
AND THE STRENGTH OF HIS POWER;
NOT ONE IS MISSING.
Isaiah 40:26

The American statistician, George Gallup (1901–1984), knew his numbers: "I could prove God statistically! Take the human body alone. The chance that all the functions of the individual would just happen is a statistical monstrosity!"

Abi May

Science has its explanations for how children come into being, but when you first hold your baby and look into those little eyes, you know that you are holding a miracle. You are looking at one of the great mysteries of the universe—a glimpse of heaven and the creative power of God. There in your arms is tangible proof of the love God has for you, for He has chosen you to parent a new soul.

Derek and Michelle Brookes

You formed my inward parts;
You covered me in my mother's womb.
I will praise You, for I am fearfully and wonderfully made;
Marvelous are Your works,
And that my soul knows very well.
Your eyes saw my substance, being yet unformed.
And in Your book they all were written,
The days fashioned for me,
When as yet there were none of them.

Psalm 139:13–14,16 ■

Life is a miracle

As you do not know what is the way of the wind,
Or how the bones grow in the womb of her
who is with child,
So you do not know the works of God
who makes everything.

Ecclesiastes 11:5

Easter is the celebration of an event that is beyond comprehension. A body was brutally whipped, nailed to a cross, and hoisted aloft to die an excruciating and shameful death, then pierced with a spear before being taken down from the cross and wrapped tightly in grave clothes, and laid in a tomb. Three days later, that same body was once more living, breathing, walking, talking.

There is another miracle beyond my comprehension, one that takes place daily. A sperm joins with an egg to form a single cell, smaller than a grain of salt. This one cell contains the complex genetic blueprint for every detail of human development, including the child's gender, hair and eye color, height, skin tone, and much more.

Within four days, the fertilized egg has traveled into the womb.

At three weeks, the foundations of the brain, spinal cord, and nervous system are established, and the heart begins to beat.

At one month, arms, legs, eyes, and ears have begun to show. The heart is pumping blood through the circulatory system.

By six weeks, the rapidly developing brain begins to control movement of muscles and organs.

At week nine, the developing life is now called a "fetus"—Latin for "young one."

At three months, the baby is perfectly formed. He has fingernails and toenails, and he can raise his eyebrows, wrinkle his forehead, and turn his head.

At 16 weeks, the baby is a little over one third the size he will be at birth.

At five months, the baby's hair, eyelashes, and nails are growing.

The rest of the time in the womb will be spent in preparation for birth, which is usually at 40 weeks, although nowadays babies born at even as little as 22 weeks have a chance of survival.

Finally comes the grand exit from the security of the womb into the world. All of the possibilities, pleasures, and pains that life brings have begun for yet another human being.

How can a single cell grow into a fully formed baby in nine months? The process can be observed, but I can no more comprehend the spark that drives that process than I can comprehend the miraculous resurrection of Jesus.

But we don't have to understand. We can simply rejoice in the wonderful gift of life that the Creator has bestowed upon us—life here in this world, and eternal life in the world beyond!

Abi May ■

My special creation

THEN THE WORD OF THE LORD CAME TO ME, SAYING:
"BEFORE I FORMED YOU IN THE WOMB I KNEW YOU;
BEFORE YOU WERE BORN I SANCTIFIED YOU."
Jeremiah 1:4–5

I remember when I formed you. With great care and special attention I handpicked each talent, each gift, each characteristic, each fiber of your being, until the combination and proportions were exactly right and each was perfectly in sync to accomplish My purpose.

I also remember the moment when I breathed into you the breath of life. Love welled up so intensely inside Me that I could not contain it, for I knew the joy you would bring to Me and those whose lives you would touch while on the great journey of life.

My eye has been on you from the very beginning. I have been with you every step of the way. I have watched you. I have loved you. I have cared for you. You have never been out of My sight.

I love you from everlasting to everlasting. Listen to My voice in your heart, and I will show you of My great, great love for you—

love which is greater than the ocean, love which stretches further than the horizon, love which the whole universe with all its stars and galaxies cannot contain, love which stretches beyond understanding into infinity and eternity!

A message from Jesus received in prayer

Our birth is but a sleep and a forgetting;
The soul that rises with us, our life's star,
Hath had elsewhere its setting,
And cometh from afar:
Not in entire forgetfulness,
And not in utter nakedness,
But trailing clouds of glory do we come
From God, who is our home.
William Wordsworth ∎

Paul's prayer

For this reason I bow my knees to the Father of our Lord Jesus Christ, from whom the whole family in heaven and earth is named, that He would grant you, according to the riches of His glory, to be strengthened with might through His Spirit in the inner man, that Christ may dwell in your hearts through faith; that you, being rooted and grounded in love, may be able to comprehend with all the saints what is the width and length and depth and height—to know the love of Christ which passes knowledge; that you may be filled with all the fullness of God. Now to Him who is able to do exceedingly abundantly above all that we ask or think, according to the power that works in us, to Him be glory in the church by Christ Jesus to all generations, forever and ever. Amen.

Ephesians 3:14–21 ∎

There is abundant evidence that
the Bible, though written by men,
is not the product of the human
mind. By countless multitudes
it has always been revered as a
communication to us from the
Creator of the universe.

Sir Ambrose Fleming

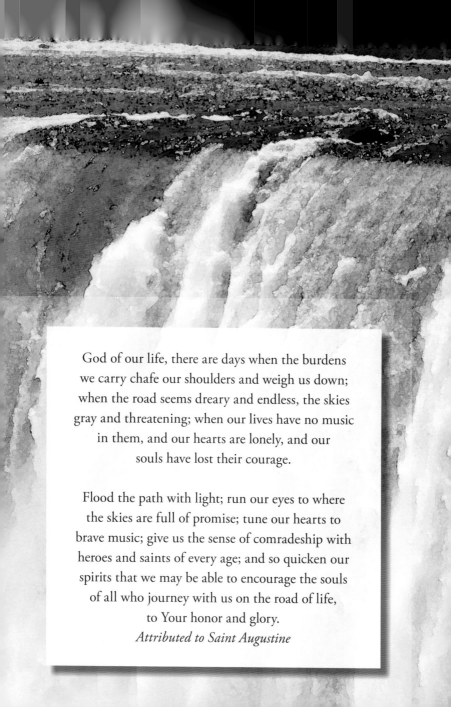

God of our life, there are days when the burdens
we carry chafe our shoulders and weigh us down;
when the road seems dreary and endless, the skies
gray and threatening; when our lives have no music
in them, and our hearts are lonely, and our
souls have lost their courage.

Flood the path with light; run our eyes to where
the skies are full of promise; tune our hearts to
brave music; give us the sense of comradeship with
heroes and saints of every age; and so quicken our
spirits that we may be able to encourage the souls
of all who journey with us on the road of life,
to Your honor and glory.
Attributed to Saint Augustine

Tell me, if you know all this

Where were you when I laid the foundations of the earth?
Tell Me, if you have understanding.
Who determined its measurements?
Surely you know!
Or who stretched the line upon it?
To what were its foundations fastened?
Or who laid its cornerstone,
When the morning stars sang together,
And all the sons of God shouted for joy?

Or who shut in the sea with doors,
When it burst forth and issued from the womb;
When I made the clouds its garment,
And thick darkness its swaddling band;
When I fixed My limit for it,
And set bars and doors;
When I said,
"This far you may come, but no farther,
And here your proud waves must stop!"

Have you commanded the morning since your days began,
And caused the dawn to know its place?
Have you entered the springs of the sea?
Or have you walked in search of the depths?
Have you comprehended the breadth of the earth?
Tell Me, if you know all this.

Where is the way to the dwelling of light?
And darkness, where is its place,
That you may take it to its territory,
That you may know the paths to its home?
Do you know it, because you were born then,
Or because the number of your days is great?

Have you entered the treasury of snow,
Or have you seen the treasury of hail,
Who has divided a channel for the overflowing water,
Or a path for the thunderbolt,
To cause it to rain on a land where there is no one,
A wilderness in which there is no man;
To satisfy the desolate waste,
And cause to spring forth the growth of tender grass?

Can you bind the cluster of the Pleiades,
Or loose the belt of Orion?
Can you bring out Mazzaroth in its season?
Or can you guide the Great Bear with its cubs?
Do you know the ordinances of the heavens?
Can you set their dominion over the earth?
Job 38:4–12,16,18–22,25–27,31–33

This most beautiful system of sun, planets, and comets
could only proceed from the counsel and dominion
of an intelligent and powerful being.
Sir Isaac Newton ■

CHAPTER 5

Taking an Upward Look

PRAISE THE LORD!
FOR IT IS GOOD TO SING PRAISES TO OUR GOD;
FOR IT IS PLEASANT, AND PRAISE IS BEAUTIFUL.
HE HEALS THE BROKENHEARTED
AND BINDS UP THEIR WOUNDS.
HE COUNTS THE NUMBER OF THE STARS;
HE CALLS THEM ALL BY NAME.
SING TO THE LORD WITH THANKSGIVING;
SING PRAISES ON THE HARP TO OUR GOD.

Psalm 147:1,3–4,7

There are always flowers for those who want to see them.
Henri Matisse

It is no use to grumble and complain;
It's just as cheap and easy to rejoice;
When God sorts out the weather and sends rain—
Why, rain's my choice.
James Whitcomb Riley

When we know that everything has two sides,
let us look at the bright side only.
Mahatma Gandhi

You say grace before meals. All right. But I say grace before
the concert and the opera, and grace before the play and
pantomime, and grace before I open a book, and grace before
sketching, painting, swimming, fencing, boxing, walking,
playing, dancing and grace before I dip the pen in the ink.
G. K. Chesterton ∎

Giving thanks

WHY ARE YOU CAST DOWN, O MY SOUL?
AND WHY ARE YOU DISQUIETED WITHIN ME?
HOPE IN GOD, FOR I SHALL YET PRAISE HIM
FOR THE HELP OF HIS COUNTENANCE.

Psalm 42:5

Our vocabulary, the way we label things and the way we express things, has a major bearing on the way we think. It would be pretty hard, for example, to think of someone whose nickname was "Pea Brain" as being intelligent and capable. If we want to think positively, we need to speak positively.

It's not wrong to ask the Lord to change a situation—the weather, for example—if we need or want it to be changed. If something hurts or hinders, we know the Lord can alter the situation in answer to our prayer. But until it happens—and even if it doesn't happen—we should maintain a positive outlook, speak positively, and thank God for what He has given us.

So even though we may not be thrilled about the rain, for example, we can still be happy in knowing that each day He gives us is "the day which the Lord has made," which is why we can "rejoice and be glad in it."[1]

"In everything give thanks."[2] In other words, in every situation give thanks. You can say, "Even though this situation is far from ideal, we thank You for all we do have and for giving us another day of life."

How can we say something is bad if it teaches us to pray or we learn lessons of faith or patience or perseverance or love—if the good effect is greater than the bad effect? Almost everything in life has its pros and cons. But if the positive outweighs the negative, then we can and should say that it is a good thing—and for those of us who love and trust God, that includes everything because in the long run He always makes the good outweigh the bad for us. "All things work together for good to those who love God."[3]

Maria Fontaine ■

[1] Psalm 118:24

[2] 1 Thessalonians 5:18

[3] Romans 8:28

THEREFORE MY HEART IS GLAD, AND MY GLORY REJOICES.

Psalm 16:9

The following is a true story about a gracious, legally blind 92-year-old woman named Maurine Jones. It seems Maurine discovered one of the secrets to happiness years ago. After Maurine's husband of 70 years passed away, she moved into a nursing home. Cheri Pape, who went along to help Maurine make the transition, tells about that day.

"After waiting patiently in the nursing home lobby for hours, Maurine smiled sweetly when told that her room was ready. As she maneuvered her walker to the elevator, I provided a visual description of her tiny room, including the eyelet curtains that had been hung on her window."

"I love it," she stated with the enthusiasm of an eight-year-old having just been presented with a new puppy.

"Mrs. Jones, you haven't seen the room. ... Just wait."

"That doesn't have anything to do with it!" she replied.
"Happiness is something you decide on ahead of time. Whether I like my room or not doesn't depend on how the furniture is arranged—it's how I arrange my mind. I already decided to love it.

"It's a decision I make every morning when I wake up. I have a choice. I can spend the day in bed recounting the difficulty I have with the parts of my body that no longer work, or I can get out of bed and be thankful for the ones that do. Each day is a gift, and as long as my eyes open I'll focus on the new day and all the happy memories I've stored away."

Attitude is everything, and as Maurine demonstrates, our attitudes don't have to be dictated by circumstances. We each have a choice.

Keith Phillips ■

Quiet Moments for Busy Days

Wheels of progress

I WILL BE GLAD AND REJOICE IN YOUR MERCY,
FOR YOU HAVE CONSIDERED MY TROUBLE;
YOU HAVE KNOWN MY SOUL IN ADVERSITIES.

Psalm 31:7

There are cycles in life—times in which everything seems to go well, and times when things seem to go badly. I want you to learn to hold on to Me through each phase of the cycle.

When you are faced with a new obstacle or problem, don't let it discourage you and don't worry that you and I together won't be able to overcome it. We will, but you must pass through this low phase of the cycle in the process. Problems cause you to exercise your faith as you rise up to meet them, and that brings the next phase of the cycle: You call on Me for help, and you fight and you win and you make progress. It's like a wheel as it turns: As the top goes down, the bottom comes around to the top and the wheel carries you forward.

Each time you face a new test, you must fight once again. You take up the challenge, call on Me for help, and once again overcome and make more progress. More tests bring more victories. But if at any time you don't seek Me for the solution, if you don't take up the challenge or don't fight through to victory, you stop the cycle. You remain at the low point and there is no forward motion; you go nowhere.

So don't look at the low points in your life as defeats, but as opportunities to make forward progress. I know it's often difficult to go through these cycles, but you must in order to keep moving forward, so keep at it!

A message from Jesus received in prayer ■

Praise your way to peace
A SPIRITUAL EXERCISE

You're having a rough day. A problem came up at work. You had a low-level argument with your spouse. You received bad news: A relative's health took a turn for the worse. You broke your favorite coffee mug. The kitchen sink sprang a leak. There doesn't seem to be too much to be cheerful about, does there?

The next time your day gets you down, try this spiritual exercise.

The concept is simple. Jesus is the Prince of Peace[1] and we can enjoy no greater peace than spending time with Him. The Bible tells us a sure way to get close to Him: We can enter into His presence through thanksgiving and praise.[2]

It is through praising God, even for the difficulties we face, that we find God's joy, which gives us strength[3] to make it through them. Praise brings joy, and joy brings strength. When we praise the Lord, we're forgetting about ourselves and our problems and concerns. Our not concentrating on ourselves, but rather concentrating on Him and His goodness, brings sweet joy to our hearts. With this joy in our hearts we're no longer pulled down by our negative feelings, doubts, worries, or fears.

Find a quiet spot. It doesn't really matter where you perform this exercise, provided you know you'll be able to have 10 or 15 minutes of peace and quiet.

Now start mentally listing each of the things that bothered you today—your problems, big or small. As you list each one, direct your thoughts to Jesus and thank Him for helping you face and survive that problem—and thank Him that it wasn't worse.

Get specific. Verbalize your thanks for each of those difficulties, one by one. For instance, "Thank You, Jesus, that the problem at work was solved by lunchtime, and now I better understand my employer's expectations," or "Thank You that Grandmother manages to stay so cheerful in spite of her illness, thank You that she has such a competent doctor, and thank You for how You are caring for her during this time"—and so on.

Do that, and you'll start feeling better very quickly! Now take a few minutes to thank Him for the good things that happened today. Think back over your day chronologically, and you'll probably be amazed to see how many good things you experienced!

This is a great exercise to perform daily, and not only when you're having a rough day. Make it a habit to praise God for everything in your life—the good and bad, the pretty and ugly, the joyous and sad—and you will experience peace and contentment.

Abi May ∎

[1] Isaiah 9:6

[2] Psalm 100:4

[3] Nehemiah 8:10

A prayer of thanksgiving

Jesus, thank You for life and all it involves. When something goes wrong, we often say, "That's life!" But life is so much more than the little things that don't turn out the way we wish they had.

Waking up each morning with eyes that see and ears that hear—that's life!

Talking with a child and catching a glimpse of the world through those innocent eyes—that's life!

Pausing in the middle of a hectic day to watch a bird soar or a butterfly flit among the flowers—that's life!

Chatting with an old friend and remembering just how special that friendship is—that's life!

Receiving an unexpected word of encouragement—that's life!

Holding a newborn baby and catching his first smile—that's life!

Walking in nature, taking in its sights and sounds, and breathing that fresh air—that's life!

Lying down to sleep at night and thanking God for all the blessings that the day brought—that's life!

Bonita Hele ■

CHAPTER 6

Resting upon God's Unchanging Love

WHO SHALL SEPARATE US FROM THE LOVE OF CHRIST?
SHALL TRIBULATION, OR DISTRESS, OR PERSECUTION, OR
FAMINE, OR NAKEDNESS, OR PERIL, OR SWORD?
YET IN ALL THESE THINGS WE ARE MORE THAN CONQUERORS
THROUGH HIM WHO LOVED US.
FOR I AM PERSUADED THAT NEITHER DEATH NOR LIFE, NOR
ANGELS NOR PRINCIPALITIES NOR POWERS, NOR THINGS
PRESENT NOR THINGS TO COME, NOR HEIGHT NOR DEPTH,
NOR ANY OTHER CREATED THING, SHALL BE ABLE TO
SEPARATE US FROM THE LOVE OF GOD WHICH IS IN CHRIST
JESUS OUR LORD.
Romans 8:35,37–39

Does Jesus care when my heart is pained
Too deeply for mirth or song,
As the burdens press, and the cares distress
And the way grows weary and long?

Does Jesus care when my way is dark
With a nameless dread and fear?
As the daylight fades into deep night shades,
Does He care enough to be near?

Oh yes, He cares, I know He cares,
His heart is touched with my grief;
When the days are weary, the long nights dreary,
I know my Savior cares.
Frank E. Graeff ■

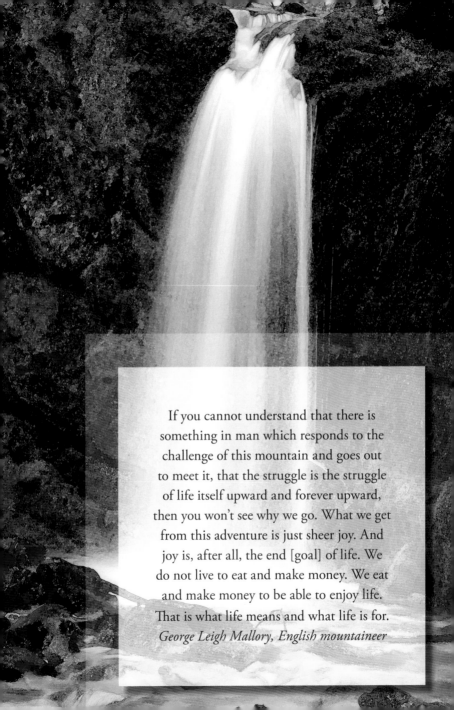

If you cannot understand that there is something in man which responds to the challenge of this mountain and goes out to meet it, that the struggle is the struggle of life itself upward and forever upward, then you won't see why we go. What we get from this adventure is just sheer joy. And joy is, after all, the end [goal] of life. We do not live to eat and make money. We eat and make money to be able to enjoy life. That is what life means and what life is for.

George Leigh Mallory, English mountaineer

A man who was completely
innocent offered himself as
a sacrifice for the good of
others, including his enemies,
and became the ransom of the
world. It was a perfect act.
Mahatma Gandhi

Up close and personal

You are special. You're not just one in a crowd—you're special to Me! I know your every thought. I know you personally, and I am speaking to you personally now. Ask Me to speak to you whenever you want, when you're up or when you're down, or even when you just want some good company. I'm happy to speak to you on any subject, whenever you need it.

Tell Me your problems and I will give you assurance, guidance, and answers. Unload on Me. I can handle any burden you place on My shoulders. I will take careful note of each concern and tenderly handle it. Be specific so I can answer you specifically. I will give you all you need, and more. Best of all, we will enjoy friendship as we spend time together.

A message from Jesus received in prayer ■

Positive affirmations

Our thoughts shape our attitude, our attitude shapes our actions, and our actions help to shape our future. A changed life begins with a change in thinking. The Bible instructs, "Be transformed by the renewing of your mind."[1] You set that process in motion by filling your mind with godly, positive thoughts. "Whatever things are true, whatever things are noble, whatever things are just, whatever things are pure, whatever things are lovely, whatever things are of good report, if there is any virtue and if there is anything praiseworthy— meditate on these things … and the God of peace will be with you."[2]

The key is believing that what you are affirming is possible, because once you believe that a certain thing is possible, it is. "If you can believe, all things are possible."[3] It takes practice to focus on the positive, but in time you will see results in a happier, more secure life.

The Bible is filled with positive affirmations. As we learn to apply those to ourselves and everyday situations, we begin to see ourselves and life more as God does, and that is reflected in our thoughts and behavior.

- Whether or not I feel capable of this task, I am going to do my best and trust Jesus to do the rest: "I can do all things through Christ who strengthens me."—*Philippians 4:13*

- I made a mistake today, but I'm determined to learn from it, get up, and try again: "The steps of a good man are ordered by the Lord, and He delights in his way. Though he fall, he shall not be utterly cast down; for the Lord upholds him with His hand."—*Psalm 37:23–24*

- I may not be perfect, but I'm special to God because He gave me a unique mind, a unique personality, unique abilities, and a unique destiny: "I am fearfully and wonderfully made; marvelous are Your works."—*Psalm 139:14*

- I have nothing to fear because God is love and He is always with me: "Perfect love casts out fear."—*1 John 4:18*

- God wants me to be happy and enjoy life: "These things I have spoken to you, that My joy may remain in you, and that your joy may be full."—*John 15:11*

- Today I'm going to think more about others and less about myself, and I'm going to make someone else's day better: "It is more blessed to give than to receive."—*Acts 20:35*

- I am not going to give up! I refuse to call it quits! Jesus promised that His strength is there for me as long as I keep trying: "Let us not grow weary while doing good, for in due season we shall reap if we do not lose heart."—*Galatians 6:9*

- I may not have as much materially as some people, but I have things that matter more—integrity and peace of mind: "Godliness with contentment is great gain."—*1 Timothy 6:6*

- God wants to guide me through today and help me make the very most of it: "Call to Me, and I will answer you, and show you great and mighty things, which you do not know." —*Jeremiah 33:3*

- God will help me make the right decisions: "If any of you lacks wisdom, let him ask of God, who gives to all liberally and without reproach, and it will be given to him."—*James 1:5*

Samuel Keating ∎

[1] Romans 12:2

[2] Philippians 4:8–9

[3] Mark 9:23

At the end of the day
A SPIRITUAL EXERCISE

I AM WITH YOU ALWAYS.
Matthew 28:20

The day is coming to a close. You're tired, perhaps even drained from all that you've needed to take care of through the long hours. Sit still for a moment or lie back in your bed. Read this message from Jesus, then close your eyes and reflect on it. Let Jesus soothe your nerves, relax your tired body, and fill your spirit with His love and peace.

"I was with you today as you worked. I was right there pulling, pushing, lifting, and carrying right along with you. I was right there doing My part to make your day that much better, your load that much lighter, and your burdens more bearable. I was there propping you up and giving you the boost you needed toward the end of the day when weariness was about to overcome you.

"I am still here with you, now when you are tired and worn from the day. Lie back and relax. Rest in My arms, like a little child falls asleep in the strong and comforting arms of her father. There is nothing to fear and nothing to worry about—only deep, sweet, peaceful rest when you are nestled here, close to My heart."[1]

Abi May ■

---

[1] A message from Jesus received in prayer

The light of your love

NOW WHEN [JESUS] ROSE EARLY ON THE FIRST DAY OF THE WEEK,
HE APPEARED FIRST TO MARY MAGDALENE.
Mark 16:9

I saw how You stooped to lift a child,
Watched how You gently, kindly smiled.
That's when I knew how much I wanted
To be part of You.

I saw how You mended broken lives,
Felt how You cared and sympathized,
Saw how their heartaches made You cry,
And I loved the heart of You.

And all of my hopes, my dreams, my fears,
Seem to dissolve within Your tears,
And I longed to hold You near
And tell You I loved You.

And all of life's cruel and stinging trials
Vanished before Your gentle smile.
That's when I knew my heart's desire
Was to spend my life walking in the light of Your love.

And when You held my upturned face,
Tenderly dried my tears away,
All of my past Your love erased,
And I was born anew.

Then I saw what it cost You to be free;
I wept as I watched You die for me.
That's when I knew that I would be
Forever in love with You.

And when You rose again and came to me,
I knew Your love was for all eternity,
And You would come one day and take me
To be with You.

And in that land of no more tears,
And in that time beyond all years,
You would embrace me, hold me near,
And tell me You loved me.

Where all of life's cruel and stinging trials
Vanish beneath Your radiant smile,
And You fulfill my heart's desire,
And I'll be there forever living in the light of Your love.
Michael Dooley ■

God's love for you is unconditional. No matter how weak or disheartened you may feel right now, or disappointed in yourself or others, He still loves you. His great, perfect, marvelous, unconditional love is not lessened, no matter what the circumstances or conditions. He keeps pouring it on and pouring it on without measure and without limit. His love is so beautiful!

Maria Fontaine ■

CHAPTER 7

Life's Tapestry

IF WRINKLES MUST BE WRITTEN UPON YOUR BROW,
LET THEM NOT BE WRITTEN UPON YOUR HEART.
THE SPIRIT SHOULD NOT GROW OLD.
James Garfield

What matters is not to add years to your life
but to add life to your years.
Alexis Carrel

The heart that loves is always young.
Johann Wolfgang von Goethe

A man's age is something impressive; it sums up his life: maturity reached slowly and against many obstacles, illnesses cured, griefs and despairs overcome, and unconscious risks taken; maturity formed through so many desires, hopes, regrets, forgotten things, loves. A man's age represents a fine cargo of experiences and memories.

Antoine de Saint-Exupéry

Age is opportunity no less
Than youth itself, though in another dress;
And as the evening twilight fades away,
The sky is filled with stars, invisible by day.

Henry Wadsworth Longfellow

Growing old is no more than a bad habit which
a busy person has no time to form.

André Maurois

Nobody grows old by merely living a number of years. People grow old only by deserting their ideals. Years may wrinkle the skin, but to give up interest wrinkles the soul. Worry, doubt, self-distrust, fear, and despair—these are the long, long years that bow the head and turn the growing spirit back to dust. You are as young as your faith, as old as your doubt; as young as your self-confidence, as old as your fear; as young as your hope, as old as your despair.

Samuel Ullman ∎

Your turn to love

Do you have parents, grandparents, or other loved ones who are suffering from any of the long-term troubles that occur naturally in old age? Here are five ways that you can return their love and support:

1. Empathize.

Put yourself in their place. You may think you have problems, but if you stop to think about what it might be like to be their age, that would probably give you a much greater appreciation for what some elderly go through.

Depending on their circumstances, they may worry about what will happen if their condition worsens and they don't have anyone to take care of them, or they may dread becoming a burden to others.

Understanding and sympathy go a long way in easing those hardships and alleviating those fears.

2. Take an interest.

Some seniors may not be as strong or sharp as they once were, but the intangibles that matter most, those personal qualities that make them the unique people they are, have not diminished. In fact, it is often in the later years that qualities such as love, thoughtfulness, loyalty, humility, humor, optimism, and wisdom come to full fruition.

That makes seniors some of the most fascinating people in the world. So does the fact that they have lived through times that those who are younger can never experience firsthand. Take the time to unearth their latent treasures, and you'll be surprised at what you'll find. They may even surprise themselves.

3. Show love and appreciation.

Sometimes simply knowing that we are loved can make all the difference in how we view and deal with our present circumstances. Knowing that they are appreciated for past efforts can also help seniors put their lives in perspective and counter feelings of regret over failures and shortcomings, both real and imagined.

Some of the saddest words ever spoken are heard at funerals: "I hope he knew how much he meant to me," or, "I wish I'd told her more often how much I loved her." Show love and appreciation while you can.

4. Help them stay active.

Numerous studies have shown that physical activity slows the aging process, which results in both prolonged life and improved quality of life. Asked why they aren't more active physically and intellectually, many seniors say it's because they don't have anyone with whom they can exercise or engage in mentally challenging activities. Help them stay active, and you will be investing in your own future at the same time.

5. Pray for them.

It has been said that praying for others is not the least we can do for them, but the most. Prayer moves the heart and hand of God to take action according to our requests, to do things that we couldn't possibly do ourselves. "Things which are impossible with men are possible with God."[1]

Prayer opens a two-way channel of communication between us and God, and it works both ways. When we're asking God for His ear, it's easier for Him to get ours. Some of His most immediate answers to our prayers come when He is able to involve us.

The very fact that you pray for others shows that you're concerned about their happiness and well-being, and this puts you in a position to better understand His loving plan for their lives and how you can help bring it to pass. When you pray for someone to not be lonely, for example, God may give you some ideas as to how you can help alleviate that loneliness—perhaps a visit or an afternoon out together, or a phone call, email, or card.

Casey Parker

Far be it from me that I should sin against the LORD
in ceasing to pray for you.
1 Samuel 12:23 ∎

[1] Luke 18:27

Let Me touch you

THERE WAS A WOMAN WHO HAD A SPIRIT OF INFIRMITY EIGHTEEN
YEARS, AND WAS BENT OVER AND COULD
IN NO WAY RAISE HERSELF UP.
BUT WHEN JESUS SAW HER, HE CALLED HER TO HIM AND SAID TO
HER, "WOMAN, YOU ARE LOOSED FROM YOUR INFIRMITY."
HE LAID HIS HANDS ON HER, AND IMMEDIATELY SHE WAS MADE
STRAIGHT, AND GLORIFIED GOD.
Luke 13:11–13

When I walked the earth many, many years ago, I went about doing good to all who crossed My path. I healed the sick, comforted the brokenhearted, lifted the spirits of those who were discouraged, and strengthened those who felt weak. And My love and power are the same today! I still long to touch and heal the bodies of those who suffer, and I still long to encourage the hearts of those who stoop under heavy burdens or go through difficult times. Since returning to heaven I have touched many who lifted their hearts to Me and told Me their needs, and I want to do the same for you.

All it takes on your part is faith. You simply have to believe that I, the Great Physician, can still touch and make you whole. I am just a prayer away. Tell Me about your troubles, your fears, your worries, and ask Me to help and heal you. Sometimes healing the body takes a while—I know the best time—but the healing of your heart, the gifts of peace in place of turmoil and faith in place of fear, I can give in an instant. It is something that you can't understand with your mind, but when you ask in faith and it happens, you will know that I have touched you.

A message from Jesus received in prayer ■

Love never reasons, but
profusely gives; gives, like
a thoughtless prodigal, its
all, and trembles then lest
it has done too little.
Hannah More

Lord, make me an instrument of Thy peace.

Where there is hatred, let me sow love;
Where there is injury, pardon;
Where there is doubt, faith;
Where there is despair, hope;
Where there is darkness, light;
Where there is sadness, joy.

O divine Master, grant that I
may not so much seek
To be consoled as to console,
To be understood
as to understand,
To be loved as to love;

For it is in giving
that we receive;
It is in pardoning
that we are pardoned;
It is in dying
that we are born to eternal life.

Author unknown,
often attributed to Saint Francis of Assisi

ALL THE LAW IS FULFILLED IN ONE WORD, EVEN IN THIS:
"YOU SHALL LOVE YOUR NEIGHBOR AS YOURSELF."
Galatians 5:14

People don't have to be perfect in order to deserve our love. They don't have to be faultless or easy to like or get along with. That's a good thing, because none of us are all those things all the time; none of us are perfect. God doesn't expect us to be perfect, but He does expect us to show one another love and understanding.

God's love is unconditional and strong enough and pure enough to withstand our human faults and mess-ups, which are many. We should ask Him for love that isn't contingent on us clicking with people, love that appreciates them for who they are, love that loves even when they are late or selfish or rude or unkempt or disorganized or just plain in the wrong.

Maria Fontaine ■

Lunch with God

There once was a little boy who wanted to meet God. He knew it was a long trip to where God lived, so he packed his suitcase with cookies and a few bottles of juice and started his journey.

When he had gone only a few blocks from home, he met an old man in a park. The old man was sitting by a pond, feeding the birds.

The boy sat down next to him, opened his suitcase, and was about to enjoy a drink when he noticed that the old man looked hungry. So the boy offered him a cookie.

The old man gratefully accepted, and smiled at him. His smile was so incredible that the boy wanted to see it again. So he offered him a drink.

The old man smiled at him again. The boy was delighted! They sat there all afternoon eating and smiling, but they hardly said a word.

As it grew dark, the boy realized he was tired and he got up to leave. But when he had gone only a few steps, he turned around, ran back to the old man, and gave him a hug. The old man gave him his biggest smile ever.

When the boy got home, his mother was surprised by the happy look on the boy's face. "What did you do today that made you so happy?" she asked.

"I had lunch with God," the boy replied. But before his mother could respond, he added, "And do you know what? He's got the most beautiful smile I've ever seen!"

Meanwhile, the old man, also radiant from his day in the park, returned to the home he shared with his grown son's family. The son was stunned by the look of peace on his father's face and asked, "Dad, what did you do today that made you so happy?"

"I ate cookies in the park with God," the old man answered. But before his son had a chance to respond, he added, "You know, He's much younger than I expected."

Too often we underestimate the power of a touch, a smile, a kind word, a listening ear, an honest compliment, or the smallest act of caring—all of which have the potential to make someone's day a very special one, or even turn someone's life around.

Author unknown ∎

CHAPTER 8

Promises and Promiser

O LORD, YOU HAVE SEARCHED ME AND KNOWN ME.
YOU KNOW MY SITTING DOWN AND MY RISING UP;
YOU UNDERSTAND MY THOUGHT AFAR OFF.
YOU COMPREHEND MY PATH AND MY LYING DOWN,
AND ARE ACQUAINTED WITH ALL MY WAYS.
FOR THERE IS NOT A WORD ON MY TONGUE,
BUT BEHOLD, O LORD, YOU KNOW IT ALTOGETHER.
YOU HAVE HEDGED ME BEHIND AND BEFORE,
AND LAID YOUR HAND UPON ME.

Psalm 139:1–5

I am here to help

I know all about you—your gifts, your talents, your strengths. I also know your weaknesses, your idiosyncrasies, and all the funny things about you that make you an individual. I know about the nagging problems that you can't seem to overcome and all the things about yourself that bother you. I know your heart's desires and secret longings. There is nothing hidden from Me.

I care about each of your disappointments and heartbreaks. I care about how you feel. I care about what you think. I care about the difficulties and hardships that you face. I care about your health. I care about your material needs. I care about your spiritual struggles. There is not one detail of your life that does not concern Me, and I am here to help.

Every time you look up to Me, I am there. I hear your prayers, and My heart is moved with compassion. I never get tired of listening to you. I am never distant. I am never too tired or too busy for you. I never turn away. I never sleep. I never hang a "Do Not Disturb" sign on My door. I always hear and answer your prayers. Sometimes I don't answer in the way you ask Me to or think I should, and sometimes you don't see the answer immediately, but I always hear and I always answer.

A message from Jesus received in prayer ■

Contingency plans

God has a contingency plan for every possible calamity. For every worry, He has a solution at His fingertips. What's more, it's His pleasure to take care of us! He doesn't consider us an annoyance when we come to Him with our fears and worries. Rather, like the loving Father He is, He picks us up and gently says, "I understand. Why don't you leave that fear with Me, and let Me handle it for you?"[1] "God has not given us the spirit of fear," the apostle Paul wrote, "but of power and of love and of a sound mind."[2]

"Trouble at work? Nasty coworkers threatening to cause trouble for you? Don't worry! Put your will on My side and I'll take care of the problem!"

Be strong and of good courage, do not fear nor be afraid of them; for the Lord your God, He is the One who goes with you. He will not leave you nor forsake you.—Deuteronomy 31:6

"Worried about war and terrorism? Don't fear! Entrust your life and your family to Me, and I'll take care of you."

In righteousness you shall be established; you shall be far from oppression, for you shall not fear; and from terror, for it shall not come near you.—Isaiah 54:14

"Afraid of natural disasters? Worried about earthquakes, tsunamis, or hurricanes? Don't be! I've got you covered. That's the best insurance policy you could ask for!"

Therefore we will not fear, even though the earth be removed, and though the mountains be carried into the midst of the sea.—Psalm 46:2

"Are you suffering physically—perhaps even battling a life-threatening sickness? Don't be afraid. I will be with you through it all, to comfort you and hold your hand."

Yea, though I walk through the valley of the shadow of death, I will fear no evil; for You are with me; Your rod and Your staff, they comfort me.—Psalm 23:4

"Have you been wrongly accused and therefore worry about saving your reputation and future? Don't. I know the truth, and I'll make sure it comes out in the end."

Listen to Me, you who know righteousness, you people in whose heart is My law: do not fear the reproach of men, nor be afraid of their insults.
—Isaiah 51:7

"It can be a scary world out there! There's a lot of bad stuff going on. Maybe you live in a dangerous area and that worries you sometimes. Don't be afraid. If I take care of the birds and the flowers, what makes you think I won't take care of you? You're worth everything to Me."

The very hairs of your head are all numbered. Do not fear therefore; you are of more value than many sparrows.—Luke 12:7

"I see you've been worried about how to provide for your family. It's been difficult to make ends meet, and the bills are piling up. Don't be afraid. The world and all that is in it are Mine, and it is My pleasure to meet every one of your needs. Just ask."

Do not fear, little flock, for it is your Father's good pleasure to give you the kingdom.—Luke 12:32

Marie Péloquin ∎

[1] 1 Peter 5:7

[2] 2 Timothy 1:7

What of Jesus himself?

THERE ARE ALSO MANY OTHER THINGS THAT JESUS DID, WHICH IF THEY WERE WRITTEN ONE BY ONE, I SUPPOSE THAT EVEN THE WORLD ITSELF COULD NOT CONTAIN THE BOOKS THAT WOULD BE WRITTEN.

John 21:25

Dozens of ancient non-biblical manuscripts confirm that Jesus was a genuine historical figure who lived in Palestine in the early part of the first century. The Encyclopedia Britannica states:

"These independent accounts prove that in ancient times even the opponents of Christianity never doubted the historicity of Jesus, which was disputed for the first time—and on inadequate grounds— by several authors during the 19th and at the beginning of the 20th centuries."[1]

For instance, the Roman historian Cornelius Tacitus mentions "Christus" in his annals published around 115 AD:

"Nero fastened the guilt and inflicted the most exquisite tortures on a class hated for their abominations, called Christians by the populace. Christus, from whom the name had its origin, suffered the extreme penalty during the reign of Tiberius at the hands of one of our procurators, Pontius Pilatus."[2]

Another example is Lucian of Samosatam, a Greek satirist who lived during the second century. He was scornful of Christians, but nevertheless his writings attest to the spread of Christianity at that time:

"The Christians ... worship a man to this day—the distinguished personage who introduced this new cult, and was crucified on that account. ... You see, these misguided creatures start with the general conviction that they are immortal for all time, which explains their contempt for death and self devotion ... their lawgiver [taught] they are all brothers, from the moment that they are converted, and deny the gods of Greece, and worship the crucified sage, and live after his laws. All this they take on faith."[3]

Abi May ∎

[1] *Encyclopedia Britannica* (1980), Vol. 10, page 145

[2] *Annals* 15.44.2-8

[3] *The Passing Peregrinus*

One who knows Him

A friend and I happened to walk past a cinema just as several movies ended and hundreds of people flooded onto the sidewalk. One man stood out in the crowd—literally—and he was walking straight toward us. He must have been seven feet tall and had the athletic build of a basketball player. As I turned to tell Abi what I was thinking, she ran up to him.

"Francisco, let me shake your hand!" she said excitedly. "No, let me hug you! You are doing such a good job! I think your team will win the championship!"

Abi's enthusiastic reaction stood out in the crowd. Everyone else seemed to ignore him. Many didn't even see the seven-foot man in their midst. They were lost in their own worlds. Out of hundreds, only Abi ran to him, greeted him by name, knew his accomplishments, and praised him for the good basketball season that he and the San Antonio Spurs were having. Being the avid sports fan she is, Abi talked about it all the way home. That moment had made her day.

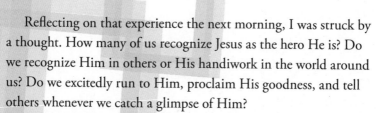

Reflecting on that experience the next morning, I was struck by a thought. How many of us recognize Jesus as the hero He is? Do we recognize Him in others or His handiwork in the world around us? Do we excitedly run to Him, proclaim His goodness, and tell others whenever we catch a glimpse of Him?

Those of us who know Jesus can see Him walking among us. We are thrilled by His presence and are changed. He may not appear as a seven-foot-tall basketball player. He may appear as a baby whose smile turns your day around. He may appear as a friend who knows the perfect word to say. He may appear as a doctor who deftly mends your broken body. He may come to you as a friendly stranger who tells you that Jesus loves you and wants to come into your heart.

Those of us who know Him love Him. We can't contain our excitement whenever we see Him, and we want others to know Him, too.

Joyce Suttin ■

CHAPTER 9

What a Wonderful World

THE FLOWERS APPEAR ON THE EARTH;
THE TIME OF SINGING HAS COME,
AND THE VOICE OF THE TURTLEDOVE
IS HEARD IN OUR LAND.
Song of Solomon 2:12

Praise the LORD!
Praise the Lord from the heavens;
Praise Him in the heights!
Praise Him, all His angels;
Praise Him, all His hosts!
Praise Him, sun and moon;
Praise Him, all you stars of light!
Praise Him, you heavens of heavens,
And you waters above the heavens!
Let them praise the name of the LORD,
For He commanded and they were created.
He also established them forever and ever;
He made a decree which shall not pass away.

Praise the LORD from the earth,
You great sea creatures and all the depths;
Fire and hail, snow and clouds;
Stormy wind, fulfilling His word;
Mountains and all hills;
Fruitful trees and all cedars;
Beasts and all cattle;
Creeping things and flying fowl;
Kings of the earth and all peoples;
Princes and all judges of the earth;
Both young men and maidens;
Old men and children.
Let them praise the name of the LORD,
For His name alone is exalted;
His glory is above the earth and heaven.
Psalm 148:1–13

We must understand spiritual truths and apply them to our modern life. We must draw strength from the almost forgotten virtues of simplicity, humility, contemplation, and prayer. It requires a dedication beyond science, beyond self, but the rewards are great and it is our only hope.

Charles Lindbergh

Prayer is the most powerful form of energy that
one can generate. The influence of prayer on
the human mind and body is as demonstrable
as that of secreting glands. Its results can be
measured in terms of increased buoyancy, greater
intellectual vigor, moral stamina and a deeper
understanding of human relationships. Only in
prayer do we achieve that complete harmonious
assembly of mind, body and spirit which gives
the frail human need its unshakable strength.

When we pray we link ourselves with the
inexhaustible motive that spins the universe.

Alexis Carrel

You visit the earth and water it,
You greatly enrich it;
The river of God is full of water;
You provide their grain,
For so You have prepared it.
You water its ridges abundantly,
You settle its furrows;
You make it soft with showers,
You bless its growth.

You crown the year with Your goodness,
And Your paths drip with abundance.
They drop on the pastures of the wilderness,
And the little hills rejoice on every side.
The pastures are clothed with flocks;
The valleys also are covered with grain;
They shout for joy, they also sing.
Psalm 65:9–13 ■

The Great Masters

It had been some years since my husband and I had spent a winter in England, and it was turning out to be a very cold, windy, and damp one. We were in the habit of walking daily for exercise, but the prospect of walking in bone-chilling weather for weeks on end was not a pleasant one. Then one day, while strolling in the city, we came upon a way to escape the cold—a visit to the National Gallery in Trafalgar Square. The more than 2,300 paintings that line the long corridors comprise the largest collection of western European art in the world and are open to the public.

Unbundling ourselves, we were glad to resume our stroll in the warmth of the gallery. We were soon captivated by the portraits and landscapes, flowers, and flocks. Such a variety of subjects and styles! It was easy to see why these artists are known as the Great Masters. The vibrant golden sunflowers of Vincent Van Gogh, the portraits of Rembrandt that seemed alive enough to step off the canvas and join our stroll, the gentle landscapes of John Constable, the softly colored gardens of Monet, and so much more. We became witnesses to the endeavors of men who had at their disposal small quantities of paint, a few paintbrushes, and a lot of talent. It was breathtaking to view, and the small plaques that accompanied each work, describing the artist's intent and technique, were fascinating to read.

Weeks passed and the weather gradually improved. The parks of London came back to life as crocuses peeked up timidly to greet the first sunshine in months. Soon daffodils trumpeted the arrival of spring in an array of yellows and golds. Trees and shrubs budded, and the grass reverted to a rich green. Even the smallest daisy, with its tiny golden heart and delicate white petals, had its particular beauty. Walks became increasingly pleasurable as the weeks progressed. As spring turned to summer, the parks were awash in color. Birds sang, butterflies fluttered through the flowers, ducklings paddled after their mothers, swans stretched their elegant necks. This too was art—a living art that varied from day to day, an art that went beyond the visual to envelop us in sounds and scents.

What intent and skill had created such beauty? I can't believe that this all came about by chance. The masterpieces of the National Gallery were not produced by random splashes of paint on canvas; they were thoughtfully designed and skillfully executed. They were not the products of chance any more than the wondrous world around us was the result of random events. I agree with the Psalmist—"The heavens declare the glory of God; and the firmament shows His handiwork".[1] God is the Greatest Master of them all!

Abi May ■

[1] Psalm 19:1

Just sing!

OH, THAT I HAD WINGS LIKE A DOVE!
I WOULD FLY AWAY AND BE AT REST.

Psalm 55:6

I was awakened early by a choir of birds. Singing, chirping, chanting, chiming, and conversing, their melodies were loud, joyful, and everywhere—nature's own surround sound. Some friends and I were camping in a wooded area near Mostar, the 600-year-old city that was often in the news during the Yugoslav Wars of the early 1990s.

The birds' notes rose in pitch and volume, then swung to a whisper, then reached a crescendo again, victorious, full of inspiration and joy. The difficulties facing this ethnically divided country were clearly the furthest thing from their little minds. Nearly 15 years after the official end of the war, Croatian Catholics, Bosnian Muslims, and Serb Orthodox are still learning how to live in the same cities, how to work together, and how to forgive.

I went for a walk along the narrow river and took in the scene—the potholed asphalt road lined with bench frames with no seats, the bridge that had been all but destroyed, the small café without doors or glass in the windows, the flowerbeds overrun with weeds. Don't step onto the grass, I reminded myself. There could be mines! For a few moments I forgot about the birds. Why did this happen? Who was responsible for this mess?

As I neared the teetering remains of the bridge, I saw a bird on one of the rails. Could she remember? Could she have seen someone die here, or have heard the shooting?

Then the bird began to sing, and I forgot about all those questions. Her tiny body quaked as her song burst forth. The music seemed to come from all of her. The sounds poured out with such force and conviction that I wanted to sing too. She seemed to be singing about the rising sun, about a new morning, about the blue sky, about a new day full of hope, about beautiful flowers and the gentle forest, about cool, flowing, sparkling waters that wash the old away. She wasn't thinking about how she looked or her performance. She was just singing with all of her being.

I don't know how long I sat there watching her, but I forgot about everything else. I listened and sang along. I sang about the feeling of freedom I felt rising in me, about new possibilities, about new ways of looking at life, about a new day full of hope, about the beauty of creation and its gentle Creator, about a great love that washes away mistakes of the past. It felt good, it felt great, and it felt liberating.

Forget about ethnic differences. Forget about broken relationships. Forget about the other guy's mistake that never ended in an apology. Learn from the birds. With all your being, with all your strength, just sing!

Mila Govorukha ∎

A nature lover, walking with a friend along a busy city street, stopped suddenly and asked his friend, "Do you hear a cricket?"

"Of course not," his friend said with a laugh. "You could never hear a cricket above the roar of all this traffic."

"I'm sure I hear a cricket," insisted the nature lover. Turning over a stone, he uncovered the insect.

"Did you actually hear that cricket chirping above this noise?" asked his friend in astonishment.

"Certainly," said the nature lover. "I make it a habit to listen to nature, whether I am in a forest, a field, or in town. Everyone hears whatever he's listening for."

To illustrate his point, he took a coin from his pocket and he dropped it to the pavement. The two men watched as each passer-by put his hand in his pocket to see if he was the one who had dropped the coin.

What are you listening for? Gold or God? Your ears are tuned to listen for something, like a radio is tuned to receive the broadcast from a distant radio station. God's ears are tuned to hear your prayers. Are yours tuned to hear what He has to say to you?

Author unknown ∎

Rest in Me

MAY MY MEDITATION BE SWEET TO HIM;
I WILL BE GLAD IN THE LORD.

Psalm 104:34

I love it when you take time to commune with Me. There don't even have to be words, prayers, or praises involved. We can commune in spirit if you turn your thoughts toward Me and let your mind and spirit dwell there. You start out by praising Me or thinking about Me, turning your heart toward Me and meditating on My goodness to you. As you do, we will start to connect in the spirit.

It takes peace and contentment of spirit to create this link with Me. Often the connection won't happen if you are worked up or worried about other things. It's like learning to float in water. If you struggle, the balance will be upset. You will break the connection with Me, and you will "sink." But if you lie back and focus on relaxing every muscle in your body, shutting out the noise of the world, you'll find that the water holds you up perfectly. It is such a wonderful feeling!

I want you to learn how to enter that state of full relaxation of mind and body, your thoughts filled entirely with Me. That is where I can minister to your spirit more directly, guide you in important matters, and give you solutions to your problems.

A message from Jesus received in prayer ∎

Trust in the LORD, and do good;
Dwell in the land, and feed on His faithfulness.
Delight yourself also in the LORD,
And He shall give you the desires of your heart.
Commit your way to the LORD,
Trust also in Him,
And He shall bring it to pass.
He shall bring forth your righteousness as the light,
And your justice as the noonday.
Rest in the LORD, and wait patiently for Him.
Psalm 37:3–7 ■

CHAPTER 10

Eternity:
The Best Is Yet to Come

THE LORD WILL ... PRESERVE ME FOR HIS HEAVENLY KINGDOM.

2 Timothy 4:18

Bettie J. Eadie, near-death survivor and author of *Embraced by the Light*, described the world beyond thus:

"Heaven in all its glory could be summed up in one word: Christ. He is the light of creation, the joy of all life, and above all, the deepest love of our souls. To embrace Him is to embrace the meaning of life and the eternal power of God."

Helen Keller, American author and activist, also wrote of her expectation, made all the more poignant considering she was blind and deaf from infancy:

"Death is no more than passing from one room into another. But there's a difference for me, you know. Because in that other room I shall be able to see."

Abi May

The joys of heaven will surely compensate for the sorrows of earth. Hush, hush, my doubts! Death is but a narrow stream, and thou shalt soon have forded it. Time, how short—eternity, how long! Death, how brief—immortality, how endless!

Charles Spurgeon ■

A pilgrim's journey

NOW THEY DESIRE A BETTER, THAT IS, A HEAVENLY COUNTRY.
Hebrews 11:16

Australia's Indian Pacific railway line runs between Sydney on the east coast to Perth on the west coast, traversing a whole continent and connecting two oceans, the Pacific and the Indian.

For most of the 65-hour journey, the train travels through some of the most rugged and barren landscapes in the world. One section crosses the Nullarbor Plain, which is an arid, treeless plain with a moon-like landscape the color of cayenne pepper. Nothing but parched, infertile limestone soil surrounds the track and stretches endlessly into the horizon. For one stretch of 478 km (297 miles) there are no bends at all in the line; it is the longest stretch of straight railway track in the world.

A special place

IN MY FATHER'S HOUSE ARE MANY MANSIONS; IF IT WERE NOT
SO, I WOULD HAVE TOLD YOU. I GO TO PREPARE A PLACE FOR YOU.
AND IF I GO AND PREPARE A PLACE FOR YOU, I WILL COME AGAIN
AND RECEIVE YOU TO MYSELF; THAT WHERE I AM, THERE YOU
MAY BE ALSO.

John 14:2–3

When I was there on earth, I told those who loved Me that I
was going before them to prepare a place for them, that where I
am, they may be also. Since that time, I've been preparing a city
for those who love Me to come to and live with Me. Since this
place is for My special friends, I wanted it to be the best and most
wonderful place there ever was, so I have created it to be perfect
in every way. I have also made beautiful homes for them to live in,
so they can be as comfortable as possible and have everything that
their hearts could desire.

(Continued on page 121.)

If life be short, then
moderate your worldly
cares and projects; do not
cumber yourselves with
too much provision for a
short voyage.
Author unknown

If we really understood Heaven,
we would be most unhappy and
unsatisfied with life on earth. We
would rebel against our earthly
limitations. If we saw Heaven, we
could not bear this earth. That's why
Heaven is forever: we cannot bear to
leave it after we get there.

Charles L. Allen

If you have received Me as your Savior, that makes you one of My special friends, and I have such a place for you. I have reserved a corner of heaven just for you, a place where all your dreams will come true, where everything you've ever wanted will be right at your fingertips, where all those you love will be near you and you will be totally happy. This is a surprise that I have waiting for you when your earthly life is over. I can hardly wait to show you all that I've made for you and to enjoy the look on your face when I do.

You might feel you don't deserve these things. You might still be ashamed of things you've done, or you may have only just met Me, or you might feel like you haven't done much for Me. But don't worry about all that. Because I see your heart and I love you more than you could possibly know or understand, these things are My gift to you. When you give a gift to a loved one, you don't give it only because of what they do for you or because they deserve it; you give it because you love them. That's how I feel about you.

A message from Jesus received in prayer ■

Remember those connect-the-dots pictures that you drew as a child? The Bible is like that: Connect certain passages in the right sequence, and you reveal a hidden picture, a spiritual truth, a mystery of God. There are thousands of pictures between its covers. Here's a favorite of mine.

1. Romans 5:8: "God demonstrates His own love toward us, in that while we were still sinners, Christ died for us."

That's pretty extreme—dying for us. Why would Jesus do that?

2. Isaiah 53:6: "All we like sheep have gone astray; we have turned, every one, to his own way."

In other words...

3. Romans 3:23: "All have sinned and fall short of the glory of God."

Okay, so we're not perfect. Why is that such a problem?

4. Isaiah 59:2: "Your [sins] have separated you from your God."

But the good news is...

5. 1 Peter 3:18: "Christ suffered once for sins, the just for the unjust, that He might bring us [back] to God, being put to death in the flesh but made alive by the Spirit"—meaning He rose from the dead.

Good for Him, but what good does His rising from the dead do for us?

6. John 11:25: "I [Jesus] am the resurrection and the life. He who believes in Me, though he may die, he shall live."

In other words...

7. John 14:19: "Because I live, you will live also."

Which brings us back to our starting point—God loves us so much that He wants us to live in that love forever.

8. John 3:16: "For God so loved the world"—you and me—"that He gave His only begotten Son, that whoever believes in Him should not perish but have everlasting life."

Keith Phillips ■

The reward of faith

We walk life's hot, hard, dusty roads battle-weary and scarred, but we arrive in heaven triumphant. The angels blow their trumpets to herald our victory. We held on when it seemed the whole world was against us. We didn't sink when the storms of life rocked our ships. Satan attacked us on every side. He threw his worst at us, but we survived. We held on. We did our best. We believed! We won the war of faith. Henceforth is laid up for us a crown of righteousness.[1]

Several years ago when I was very ill, recovering from a bout with cancer, Jesus told me that He had given me an "angel of comfort" to be with me during those difficult times. I never saw her face, but through many long days and lonely nights, when the pain was at its worst, I could feel her presence, like a tender mother's, as though my head lay in her lap while she held me close and stroked my head.

It was such a blessed feeling of peace, like a soft, warm aura that enveloped me. In spite of the pain, I found my heart filled with wonder and thankfulness for that special touch from heaven.

I am now certain of one thing: angels are not far from us, floating around on clouds in heaven. They are here, all around us, standing ready night and day to serve, aid, comfort, and protect us. I may not be able to see them, but I know they are near.

When I receive my heavenly crown someday, I will know that I didn't earn it by myself; I was aided in my fight of faith by a "great cloud of witnesses,"[2] the invisible armies of heaven. On that glorious day I will want to meet my angel of comfort and the other dear ones who walked with me and lifted me up when I was weary. On that day, I will thank them face to face.

Misty Kay ■

[1] 1 Timothy 6:12; 2 Timothy 4:7–8
[2] Hebrews 12:1

Now I saw a new heaven and a new earth, for the first heaven and the first earth had passed away. Also there was no more sea. Then I, John, saw the holy city, New Jerusalem, coming down out of heaven from God, prepared as a bride adorned for her husband. And I heard a loud voice from heaven saying, "Behold, the tabernacle of God is with men, and He will dwell with them, and they shall be His people. God Himself will be with them and be their God. And God will wipe away every tear from their eyes; there shall be no more death, nor sorrow, nor crying. There shall be no more pain, for the former things have passed away."

Revelation 21:1–4 ■

CHAPTER 11

Oasis of Peace

CAUSE ME TO HEAR YOUR LOVINGKINDNESS IN THE MORNING,
FOR IN YOU DO I TRUST;
CAUSE ME TO KNOW THE WAY IN WHICH I SHOULD WALK,
FOR I LIFT UP MY SOUL TO YOU.

Psalm 143:8

I met God in the morning,
When the day was at its best,
And His presence came like sunrise,
Like a glory in my breast.

All day long the presence lingered,
All day long He stayed with me,
And we sailed in perfect calmness
O'er a very troubled sea.

Other ships were blown and battered.
Other ships were sore distressed.
But the winds that seemed to drive them,
Brought to me a peace and rest.

Then I thought of other mornings,
With a keen remorse of mind,
When I too had loosed the moorings,
With the presence left behind.

So, I think I know the secret,
Learned from many a troubled way:
You must seek Him in the morning
If you want Him through the day.
Ralph Spaulding Cushman ■

Six steps of meditative prayer

Now in the morning, having risen a long while before
daylight, He went out and departed to a solitary place;
and there He prayed.
Mark 1:35

Step 1: Choose an appropriate location. Most people find
that meditation is best in quiet, uncluttered surroundings, ideally
away from where they work or spend most of their waking hours. A
secluded spot outside can be especially conducive. Fresh air not only
renews us physically, but it also illustrates God's Spirit that is able to
clear our minds and spirits.

Step 2: Take time to wind down. It's impossible to immediately
go from the affairs of a busy day into a state of deep meditative
prayer. There needs to be a time of transition, a time of phasing out
the material world. Sometimes it helps to spend a few minutes on
a transitional activity, such as listening to soothing music, taking a
short walk, or breathing deeply. As you try different things, you'll
find what works best for you.

Step 3: Leave your cares at the door. If problems are weighing you down, they'll keep you from the peace you could receive from meditation. Take a minute or two (or as long as it takes) to give your present cares to Jesus in prayer. Be specific. Describe to Him what is troubling you, and ask Him to lift and bear it. Focus on God's ability to bring solutions, rather than the problems themselves. "Be anxious for nothing, but in everything by prayer and supplication, with thanksgiving, let your requests be made known to God; and the peace of God, which surpasses all understanding, will guard your hearts and minds through Christ Jesus."[1]

Step 4: Get relaxed. Several minutes of gentle stretches and deep breathing, followed by a relaxation exercise (concentrate on relaxing your face and neck, then your entire body, part by part) can help. If you're feeling especially tense, a shower or a bath or a short walk in nature might help you relax. Or if you're very tired, a nap may be just the thing, because as long as you're exhausted, you probably won't get much out of your time of meditation.

Step 5: Select a comfortable position. In meditation, the position of your spirit matters much more than the position of your body. You don't have to sit a certain way—or even sit, for that matter—except of course you should be comfortable, so that doesn't become a distraction. Whatever position you choose, it should allow you to maintain good posture, because this facilitates deep breathing and good circulation of the blood.

Step 6: Meditate. You've found an appropriate spot and wound down physically. You've put your problems and cares into Jesus' very capable hands. You've disconnected from the affairs of the day, and are relaxed and comfortable. Now you're ready to begin a time of focused meditation.

You might choose to focus on Jesus Himself, thinking about one of His attributes, or on some special blessing He has brought into your life. A specific thought from God's Word can also be a subject for meditation. Reading a passage from the Bible or some other short devotional material may help get you started.

Let your mind rest. Don't analyze. Just relax and concentrate on quieting your body, mind, and spirit. Think of this type of meditation as being like learning to float in water. It takes that amount of relaxation of both body and spirit for God's Spirit to take over and give you the "buoyancy" you need. If you struggle or try to poke your head up to see what's happening around you, the balance will be upset and you'll break your connection with Him. Whereas if you will just lie back, stop struggling, focus on relaxing every muscle in your body, and shut out the noise of the world and every thought except the one you're meditating on, God's Spirit will hold you up perfectly. It's a wonderful feeling!

"Peace I leave with you," Jesus promised. "My peace I give to you; not as the world gives, do I give to you."[2] Let Him carry you away to the peaceful haven He has prepared for you.

Alex Peterson ■

[1] Philippians 4:6–7

[2] John 14:27

Jesus, the great problem solver
A PRAYER

SUDDENLY A GREAT TEMPEST AROSE ON THE SEA, SO THAT THE
BOAT WAS COVERED WITH THE WAVES. BUT [JESUS] WAS ASLEEP.
THEN HIS DISCIPLES CAME TO HIM AND AWOKE HIM, SAYING,
"LORD, SAVE US! WE ARE PERISHING!"
BUT HE SAID TO THEM, "WHY ARE YOU FEARFUL, O YOU OF
LITTLE FAITH?" THEN HE AROSE AND REBUKED THE WINDS AND
THE SEA, AND THERE WAS A GREAT CALM.
Matthew 8:24–26

Thank You, dear Jesus, that You're the greatest problem solver. You
came to solve mankind's biggest problem—our need for salvation, to
be freed from having to pay the price for our sins. But You didn't stop
there. During Your earthly life You solved so many other problems.
When there was no wine at the wedding, You created more wine.[1]
When people came to You with their health problems, even ones
they'd had for many years, You healed them.[2] When there was no
food for the multitudes You were teaching and everyone was hungry,
You multiplied the loaves and fishes.[3] When the adulterous woman
was about to be stoned, You had a big problem on Your hands, but
with great wisdom, humility, and love You put the hypocrites in their
place and not only saved but changed the woman's life.[4]

And every day You make Yourself available to help me solve my problems. Thank You for that! I know that I'm a mess. I'm only human. I make mistakes. I say and do the wrong things at times. Sometimes I hurt others without meaning to. That's why I need Your help so much.

Please help me to see problems as challenges, not as dead ends or disasters, knowing that You're there to help and that no problem is too big for You. Thank You for how You manage to turn every problem and difficulty I face into a steppingstone to greater progress. I know You have the power to solve the problems I face today, so I call on that power now. Amen.

Maria Fontaine ■

[1] John 2:1–11

[2] Matthew 12:15; Luke 4:40

[3] Matthew 14:15–21

[4] John 8:3–11

Constant companion

GOD IS OUR REFUGE AND STRENGTH,
A VERY PRESENT HELP IN TROUBLE.
Psalm 46:1

I want to be a very present companion, counselor, and help to you—not merely someone you know of, or someone you met once but rarely think about or talk to, or even an advisor that you consult from time to time when you have a problem or need to make an important decision. I want to be a constant, loving presence.

I want to communicate with you personally and directly, and not in a distant, formal, or mental sort of way, but heart to heart. I want us to commune as intimates would, to talk things over, to reach decisions together, and to sometimes communicate without saying a word. I want to develop a bond of love between us that you've never experienced with anyone else and can't even imagine.

Learning to converse freely with Me, like learning to be natural, open, honest, and trusting in your communications with any friend, is something that comes with time and practice. It may feel awkward or even seem like work at first, learning to come into My presence and recognize My voice, but if you will do your part by making that effort, I will speak to you. At first you may think that little voice you hear deep inside is your mind, but in time you will know that it is Mine. I may give you ideas or solutions or answers to your questions, or I may give you a feeling of peace and well-being, or I may simply tell you how special you are to Me and how much I enjoy being with you. I'm full of surprises, so you'll never know what to expect, but this one thing I promise: I will never disappoint you!

A message from Jesus received in prayer ■

A 113-year-old man,
when asked the secret
of his longevity, replied,
"When it rains, I let it."
Author unknown

I will cast all my
cares on God. They
cannot burden Him.
Joseph Hall

CHAPTER 12

Life

Life is an opportunity, benefit from it.
Life is a beauty, admire it.
Life is bliss, taste it.
Life is a dream, realize it.
Life is a challenge, meet it.
Life is a duty, complete it.
Life is a game, play it.
Life is costly, care for it.
Life is wealth, keep it.
Life is love, enjoy it.
Life is mystery, know it.
Life is a promise, fulfill it.
Life is sorrow, overcome it.
Life is a song, sing it.
Life is a struggle, accept it.
Life is tragedy, confront it.
Life is an adventure, dare it.
Life is luck, make it.
Life is too precious, do not destroy it.
Life is life, fight for it!

Mother Teresa

Reinvention

"Necessity is the mother of invention," Plato wrote.[1] Others have since added that necessity is also the mother of reinvention—meaning that new challenges give birth to progress in new directions. That certainly has proven true during the economic upheavals of the past years. Forced from their relatively comfortable positions in the former status quo, many people have reinvented their businesses or found promising new careers in fields they never would have considered otherwise. Others have reexamined their priorities and are now focusing on things they used to think they didn't have much time for, such as family, community service, charity work, further education, or spiritual pursuits. If you're looking to reinvent yourself, Jesus is a master at that. The Bible promises, "If anyone is in Christ, he is a new creation; old things have passed away; behold, all things have become new."[2]

Alex Peterson ■

[1] *The Republic*, circa 380 bc

[2] 2 Corinthians 5:17

The puzzle

LEAD ME IN YOUR TRUTH AND TEACH ME,
FOR YOU ARE THE GOD OF MY SALVATION.
Psalm 25:5

From the early-learning wooden or foam variety to intricate 10,000-piece or 3D types, puzzles are a proven way to develop problem-solving skills, as well as a pleasant hobby for all ages.

When I was 11, I became fascinated with jigsaw puzzles. My mother and I would relax together at the kitchen table, piecing together increasingly complex puzzles. We would cover the unfinished puzzle with the tablecloth at mealtimes, then remove it afterward and get to work at finding that next piece.

It has been a while since I've had the time to assemble a major puzzle, but my toddler is learning to put simple ones together. I can take one look at the pieces and easily tell where they will fit, yet my little boy sometimes struggles to find the proper place for the piece he is holding. When he gets stuck and frustrated, he turns to me and I give him a suggestion or a clue. Eventually he figures out where each piece goes and is happy. I love that look of accomplishment that he gets when he has completed the puzzle.

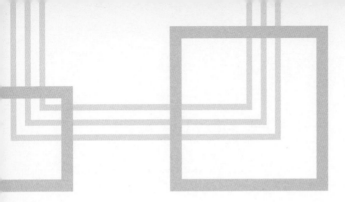

Sometimes we face complicated situations where there appears to be no way out or through. It's often during those times that we realize "resorting to prayer" is our best option. How like children we are, trying to piece together and make sense of difficult situations ourselves, when God is ready, willing, and able to help.

Like a parent, He enjoys helping us work on the puzzle of life. From His vantage point He can easily see which piece needs to go where, and what should come next. He doesn't put the puzzle together for us, because we wouldn't learn much if He did. But when we get stuck, He can give us hints. He works with us piece by piece, and piece by piece we see the picture come together.

Bonita Hele ■

Connected

MY VOICE YOU SHALL HEAR IN THE MORNING, O LORD;
IN THE MORNING I WILL DIRECT IT TO YOU,
AND I WILL LOOK UP.

Psalm 5:3

I want to be a very present help, coworker, companion, and friend as you go about your busy days. I want to make a strong connection with you first thing in the morning, and then I want to keep that connection strong all day long as we enjoy each other's company, talk things over, and work things out together.

You're in the habit of launching right into your day without making that connection, and when situations or problems arise you try to sort them out on your own, as best you can. By the time you remember to pray—if you remember at all—you've usually already decided what to do, based on your experience or what seems reasonable. Because I can see things more clearly and completely than you can, I often have a better plan, but it's hard for Me to get through to you because your own thoughts get in the way. You mean well, but things would go smoother and turn out better if you were in closer communication with Me.

So before your day begins, take a few quiet minutes with Me. Try to block from your mind all of your plans and thoughts about the day ahead and spend those few minutes reading My Word, thinking about Me, thanking Me for all I've done for you in the past, and thanking Me in advance for My continued help and blessings. As you do these things, our minds and spirits will meet. Once you've made that connection, if you will continually turn your thoughts toward Me, My love, peace, and power will carry you through the day, come what may.

A message from Jesus received in prayer ■

Psalm 23
What's in it for you?

The Lord is my shepherd.—That's relationship.
   I shall not want.—That's supply.
   He makes me to lie down in green pastures.—That's rest.
   He leads me beside the still waters.—That's refreshment.
   He restores my soul.—That's spiritual healing.
   He leads me in the paths of righteousness... —That's guidance.
   ... for His name's sake.—That's purpose.
   Yea, though I walk through the valley of the shadow of death...
   —That's tribulation.
   ... I will fear no evil... —That's protection.
   ... for You are with me.—That's faithfulness.
   Your rod and Your staff, they comfort me.—That's discipline.
   You prepare a table before me in the presence of my enemies.
   —That's hope.
   You anoint my head with oil, my cup runs over.—That's abundance.
   Surely goodness and mercy shall follow me all the days of my life.
   —That's blessing.
   And I will dwell in the house of the Lord...—That's security.
   ... forever.—That's eternity.

        David the psalmist, with comments by an unknown author ∎

Prayer for the day

YOU, WHO HAVE SHOWN ME GREAT AND SEVERE TROUBLES,
SHALL REVIVE ME AGAIN,
AND BRING ME UP AGAIN FROM THE DEPTHS OF THE EARTH.

Psalm 71:20

Jesus, I can be thankful even for the struggles in my life and the things that are difficult, because they force me to turn to You for help and You always give me the answers. You make things so clear and easy to understand. All I have to do is turn my heart to You and receive.

Without difficulties, disappointments, and failures I wouldn't have come to know Your compassion, Your understanding, and Your forgiveness, and I wouldn't be able to pass them on to others.

Thank You for all the things You bring my way to keep me humble and make me more dependent on You. Thank You for keeping me close to You. Amen. ∎

In his literary classic *Les Misérables*, Victor Hugo tells the story of Jean Valjean, whose already difficult life is brought down by one rash decision. Valjean steals a loaf of bread to feed his sister's starving children and spends the next 19 years on chain gangs and as a galley slave. Unable to find work after his release because he is an ex-convict, Valjean begs at the home of a bishop who feeds him and gives him a bed for the night. But Valjean is overcome by despair at what seems an impossibly bleak future, yields to temptation, steals some of the bishop's silver, and slips away in the night. He doesn't get far, however, before he is arrested with the silver and hauled back to face the bishop. Knowing what will happen to Valjean if he is convicted a second time, the kind bishop takes a chance on Valjean and tells the police, "I gave him the silver." Valjean is free from the law, but not his conscience. After he steals yet again, he is driven to another point of decision, and this time he makes the right one. He repents, and from that moment on he is a changed man. He goes through more upheavals and faces more tough decisions in the years that follow, but he stays true to the new course God has helped him chart.

Les Misérables is a moving portrayal of the redeeming power of God's love, but it also illustrates how our lives are shaped by our decisions. Even seemingly small decisions can have far-reaching rewards or consequences. How can we ensure that we make right decisions? The only way is to involve God in the decision-making process, because He alone knows what's best. He wants to see us make good choices and is always there to back us up when we do, so the smartest decision we can ever make is to get in the habit of asking for His help.

Keith Phillips ■

Of men and mountains

Jesus went up on the mountain, and there
He sat with His disciples.
John 6:3

Short is the little time which remains to thee of life.
Live as on a mountain.
Marcus Aurelius

The mountains will always be there,
the trick is to make sure you are too.
Hervey Voge, mountaineer

You cannot stay on the summit forever; you have to come
down again. So why bother in the first place? Just this: What
is above knows what is below, but what is below does not
know what is above. One climbs, one sees. One descends, one
sees no longer, but one has seen. There is an art of conducting
oneself in the lower regions by the memory of what
one saw higher up. When one can no longer see,
one can at least still know.
Rene Daumal

If the conquest of a great peak brings moments of exultation
and bliss, which in the monotonous, materialistic existence
of modern times nothing else can approach, it also presents
great dangers. It is not the goal of grand alpinism to face peril,
but it is one of the tests one must undergo to deserve the joy
of rising for an instant above the state of crawling grubs. On
this proud and beautiful mountain we have lived hours of
fraternal, warm, and exalting nobility. Here for a few days we
have ceased to be slaves and have really been men.
It is hard to return to servitude.
Lionel Terray, mountaineer

On the mountain, people become better.
You are closer to God and paradise.
Ulrich Inderbinen, Swiss mountain guide at 103 years old ■

CHAPTER 13

God's Word

HOLDING FAST THE WORD OF LIFE.
Philippians 2:16

Blessed are those who hear the word of God and keep it!
Luke 11:28

Let mental culture go on advancing, let the natural sciences
progress in ever greater extent and depth, and the human
mind widen itself as much as it desires—beyond the elevation
and moral culture of Christianity, as it shines
forth in the Gospels, it will not go.
Johann Wolfgang Von Goethe

All human discoveries seem to be made only for the purpose
of confirming more and more strongly the truth
contained in the sacred Scriptures.
Sir William Herschel, astronomer

The Bible is the sacred collection, preserved under the name
of Book of books, which contains the doctrinal, moral, and
religious system relatively most profound, popular, and
intelligible that has come into existence
in the history of mankind.
Francisco Giner de los Ríos, educator and philosopher

All that I think, all that I hope, all that I write, all that
I live for, is based upon the divinity of Jesus Christ,
the central joy of my poor, wayward life.
William Gladstone, British Prime Minister

In books I converse with men, in the Bible
I converse with God.
William Romaine

For me, the Bible is the Book. I cannot see how
anybody can live without it.
Gabriela Mistral, Nobel prizewinner ■

Help is here

THE LORD PASSED BY, AND A GREAT AND STRONG WIND TORE
INTO THE MOUNTAINS AND BROKE THE ROCKS IN PIECES BEFORE
THE LORD, BUT THE LORD WAS NOT IN THE WIND; AND AFTER
THE WIND AN EARTHQUAKE, BUT THE LORD WAS NOT IN THE
EARTHQUAKE; AND AFTER THE EARTHQUAKE A FIRE,
BUT THE LORD WAS NOT IN THE FIRE; AND
AFTER THE FIRE A STILL SMALL VOICE.
1 Kings 19:11–12

The Bible says that God is near to the brokenhearted[1] and a very present help in times of trouble.[2] He's more than a shoulder to cry on or a hand to hold. He can reach into the deepest places of your heart. He can soothe the pain and suffering, and replace it with His love, peace, comfort, and yes, even joy. He can do all this through His words. When He shines the light of His Word on your tears, they turn to rainbow hues. It's sunshine after the rain, light at the end of the tunnel.

Jesus loves you dearly. He wants to express that love to you, but He can't unless you let Him. He wants to tell you why He has allowed certain difficulties to befall you, but He needs you to listen. He wants to help you understand why you're feeling the way you are, and to tell you what you can do about it, but you need to want His answers. In your most trying times, His Word—His written Word and His living Word spoken directly to your mind—will come alive to you if you reach out and receive it.

Rafael Holding ∎

A smile is a light in
the window of the
soul indicating the
heart is at home.
Author unknown

You must live with people
to know their problems,
and live with God in
order to solve them.
P.T. Forsyth

The Bible—fact or fable?

Despite popular dismissals of the Bible as little more than fables and fabrication, archaeology has provided remarkable evidence of its historical accuracy. For example, the archive of the ancient city of Ebla in northern Syria was discovered in the 1970s. The documents it contained, written on clay tablets around 2300 BC, demonstrate that personal and place names in the accounts of the Hebrew patriarchs Abraham, Isaac, and Jacob are real. Ancient customs reflected in the stories of the patriarchs have also been found in clay tablets.

Another example concerns Sargon, king of Assyria, who is referred to in the book of Isaiah, but whose existence historians long disputed: "In the year that Tartan came to Ashdod, when Sargon the king of Assyria sent him, and fought against Ashdod and took it."[1] We now know that Sargon II was indeed an Assyrian king who started his reign in 722 BC. Sargon's palace at Khorsabad, Iraq, was discovered by Paul-Émile Botta in 1843. Further excavation of the site some 90 years later found the very event mentioned in Isaiah— Assyria's conquest of Ashdod—recorded on the palace walls. Visitors to the British Museum in London can see the colossal winged bull taken from the palace.

A third example was discovered in the British Museum itself. In the summer of 2007, visiting professor Michael Jursa, an Assyriologist, was searching through the museum's collection of 130,000 Assyrian cuneiform tablets when he came across a name he half remembered—Nabu-sharrussu-ukin, described there in a hand 2,500 years old as "the chief eunuch" of Nebuchadnezzar II, king of Babylon. The small tablet on which the name appears is a bill of receipt acknowledging Nabu-sharrussu-ukin's payment of about 0.75 kg of gold to a temple in Babylon.

Jursa checked the Old Testament and found the same name, rendered differently by the Bible's translators, in chapter 39 of the book of Jeremiah. Nebo-Sarsekim, according to Jeremiah, was "chief officer" to Nebuchadnezzar II and was with him at the siege of Jerusalem in 587 bc, when the Babylonians overran the city.

Dr. Irving Finkel of the British Museum summed up the significance. "This is a fantastic discovery, a world-class find. A throwaway detail in the Old Testament turns out to be accurate and true. I think that it means that the whole of the narrative [of Jeremiah] takes on a new kind of power."[2]

Abi May ∎

[1] Isaiah 20:1

[2] www.telegraph.co.uk, 13/07/07

A prayer

SEEK FIRST THE KINGDOM OF GOD AND HIS RIGHTEOUSNESS, AND
ALL THESE THINGS SHALL BE ADDED TO YOU.
Matthew 6:33

Dear Jesus, keep me from having my life so full of good things
that I don't have time for the best. Help me not to be so pressured
that I put off my time with You. Help me to bask in Your spiritual
sunshine, rest in Your arms, drink deeply of Your Word, and inhale
of Your Spirit. Help me to seek You daily and love You most of all—
more than any of the other things I enjoy. Help me to remember how
You said that without You, I can do nothing.[1] Help me to not have
misplaced priorities, but to keep You, Your love, and Your values in
the right place—first.

Maria Fontaine ■

[1] John 15:5

God's Word

An audience with Jesus

A spiritual exercise

Your [God's] words were found, and I ate them,
And Your word was to me the joy and rejoicing of my heart.
Jeremiah 15:16

Jesus said, "The words that I speak to you are spirit, and they are life!"[1] God's Word, the Bible as well as Bible-based devotional and inspirational material, nourishes our spirit and keeps us alive and healthy spiritually. Just like we have to eat in order to have physical strength, we have to feed from the Word to have spiritual strength.

The challenge that many of us face when we sit down to read is that we're too easily distracted by the thoughts of the day. Sometimes the answer lies in simply putting forth a little more effort. This spiritual exercise may help.

Next time you sit down to read God's Word, imagine that Jesus is sitting next to you. Instead of merely reading the words on the page, imagine that Jesus is personally telling you these things face to face, in a personal audience with you. He is always with you in spirit,[2] but if He were with you in bodily form, if you could see Him, you would surely be hanging on His every word.

That's how you should look at your time reading God's Word, as a personal audience with Jesus, the King of all kings, during which He is presenting you with special words of wisdom, instruction, guidance, inspiration, and encouragement.

Abi May

A skeptic and a Christian were discussing whether the Bible was truly a divinely inspired book. The skeptic was convinced that since no one had ever seen God and there was no scientific proof of His existence, how could anyone believe the Bible was truly inspired by Him?

"Is the compiler of the multiplication table known?" the Christian asked.

"No."

"Then of course you do not believe in it."

"Oh, yes, I believe in it because it works," replied the skeptic.

"So does the Bible."

Author unknown ■

[1] John 6:63

[2] Hebrews 13:5

CHAPTER 14

Making the Connection

IN QUIETNESS AND CONFIDENCE
SHALL BE YOUR STRENGTH.
Isaiah 30:15

The quieter the mind, the more powerful, the worthier, the
deeper, the more telling, and more perfect the prayer is.
Meister Eckhart

Turn your eyes upon Jesus,
Look full in His wonderful face,
And the things of earth will grow strangely dim,
In the light of His glory and grace.
Helen H. Lemmel

How brief is our span of life compared with the time since You created the universe. How tiny we are compared with the enormity of Your universe. How trivial are our concerns compared with the complexity of Your universe. How stupid we are compared with the genius of Your creation.

Yet during every minute and every second of our lives You are present, within and around us. You give Your attention to each and every one of us. Our concerns are Your concerns. And You are infinitely patient with our stupidity. I thank You with all my heart, knowing that my thanks are as nothing compared to Your greatness.

Fulbert of Chartres

Finally, brethren, whatever things are true, whatever things
are noble, whatever things are just, whatever things are pure,
whatever things are lovely, whatever things are of good report,
if there is any virtue and if there is anything praiseworthy—
meditate on these things.

Phillipians 4:8 ■

The bridge

The Lord will give strength to His people;
The Lord will bless His people with peace.
Psalm 29:11

When I moved to the port city of Tampico, Mexico, and began working with a group of volunteers, they took me for a tour of the townhouse we share. It is located fairly close to the busy downtown, but also not too far from the poorer outlying areas where we conduct most of our projects. The setting is nice, located near a beautiful lagoon where folks gather to mingle in the cooling twilight, and also just a short drive from a clean uncrowded beach.

What a terrific place! I thought, as we climbed the last flight of stairs. But the best was yet to come. A door led onto the balcony, where we were greeted by a panorama of palm trees, rooftops, and, in the distance, a magnificent bridge spanning the bay. The combination of the brightly lit spans of the bridge, the rooftops, and the cool night breeze was breathtaking, and the scene from that balcony has made for many an inspiring evening since.

The coastal weather can be changeable, sometimes calling for a thin blouse in the mid-afternoon and a warm sweater in the evening. Although it's usually sunny and clear, there have also been storms, unexpected cloudiness and rain, and some very windy conditions— occasionally even a hurricane. Whatever the weather, however, I take a few moments almost every day to stop and look out at the magnificent view from our balcony. I find the view of that beautiful bridge inspiring and somehow comforting. It connects two worlds, making all sorts of things possible that wouldn't be otherwise.

One morning as I took a few minutes for quiet reflection in one of the rooms adjoining the balcony, I looked out and expected to see the bridge, but it wasn't there. Maybe an unexpected fog or haze had rolled in and obscured the view, I thought. But I soon realized that it was my position that was off. I moved over a bit and was able to view the inspiring scene once again.

Then I was struck by a new thought—that that bridge is a lot like our relationship with God. It's always there to both inspire and comfort. By it we have access to another realm, and by it we are able to receive the help and guidance that we need. But sometimes it can seem as though the "view" is gone, or that the help we've learned to rely on has somehow failed, just this once. But actually we just need to change the position of our heart. Then that sweet inspiration and comfort and peace comes back into "view" once again, and our faith is restored.

Janet Barnes ■

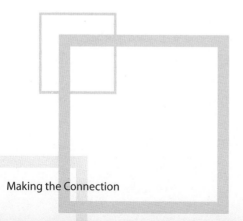
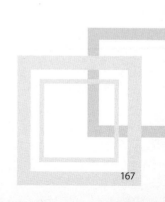

My people will dwell in a peaceful habitation,
In secure dwellings, and in quiet resting places.
Isaiah 32:18

Sometimes I just like to sit here silently with You.
You already know.
You already understand.
I don't have to say the right thing, or anything at all;
You accept me.
You see my thoughts as they form and dance.
Words could never aptly express them.
You could verbalize Your every thought perfectly,
Yet You sometimes choose silence too.
There's just something about being together,
Not having to say a thing,
Because we feel it, we sense it, we know it.
Jessie Richards

[Jesus] said to her, "Daughter, be of good cheer;
your faith has made you well. Go in peace."
Luke 8:48 ■

BE STILL, AND KNOW THAT I AM GOD.
Psalm 46:10

Some years ago I became friends with a successful young businessman named Henry. Henry was in perpetual motion, but eventually I got him to stop long enough to tell me how he had gotten where he was. During his first year of college, his father had given him some money to invest, and he had gone into business with a childhood friend. They quickly did so well that Henry doubled his class load so he could graduate a year early and go to work full time. He finished at the top of his class, with a double major. (He'd always been an overachiever, he explained.)

By the time I met him ten years later, he had made more money than a lot of people make in a lifetime, but he was still putting in fever-pitch 10- and 12-hour days. He also had an active social life. After observing this (and the inevitable toll it was taking) for a few weeks, I asked him when he found time for reflection. That came as an entirely new thought to him.

We don't have to be living in the fast lane like Henry to miss taking time to think about the deeper things of life. There are more than enough other things to keep us occupied every waking moment, but we miss the best when we fill up on things of little real consequence.

God created us with a hunger for truth and happiness and peace of mind, for total love and complete understanding. That is an inner void that He made to be filled with Himself, and only He can fill it. He wants nothing more than to do just that, and He will if we will just hold still long enough.

Keith Phillips ∎

Renewal of spirit
A SPIRITUAL EXERCISE

AS YOU HAVE THEREFORE RECEIVED CHRIST JESUS THE LORD, SO
WALK IN HIM, ROOTED AND BUILT UP IN HIM AND ESTABLISHED
IN THE FAITH, ... ABOUNDING IN IT
WITH THANKSGIVING.

Colossians 2:6–7

"If anyone is in Christ," the Bible tells us, "he is a new creation; old
things have passed away; behold, all things have become new."[1] That
transformation begins the moment we invite Jesus into our hearts
and lives, but it takes considerably longer for us to get into Jesus—to
get completely immersed in Him and grounded in faith. The more
we do that, the more of our old thoughts and habits pass away, and
the more "all things become new."

Ask God to show you one or two ways in which you need to
change or grow as a person. For example, do you generally have a
thankful, positive attitude, or do you tend to grumble about life's

difficulties? Do you set aside time to read God's Word and think about how it applies to you, or do you fill your spare moments with TV or other entertainment? Do you pray for others who are experiencing hardships, or merely think about them sympathetically? Do you cheerfully give of yourself, or resent the sacrifices you sometimes need to make for the sake of others? Or is there some other area in which you need to change?

Now take a few minutes to commit these issues to Jesus in prayer. "Create in me a clean heart, and renew a right spirit within me."[2]

It takes time and consistent effort to break old habits, but once you acknowledge the need to change and ask Jesus to help, this promise is yours: "He who has begun a good work in you will complete it."[3] As you do your part, He will do His.

Abi May ∎

[1] 2 Corinthians 5:17
[2] Psalm 51:10 (KJV)
[3] Philippians 1:6

Happiness is what we make it. Some people are unbelievably cheerful in the midst of difficulty or obstacles; others bemoan the slightest inconvenience. Those who look for the upside of any trouble are the ones who come out ahead in quality of life and the radiance of their positive attitude sheds light on the paths of others.

Chloe West

Jesus had no servants,
yet they called Him Master.
He had no degree,
yet they called Him Teacher.
He had no medicines,
yet they called Him Healer.
He had no army,
yet kings feared Him.
He won no military battles,
yet He conquered the world.
He committed no crime,
yet they crucified Him.
He was buried in a tomb,
yet He lives today.
Author unknown

CHAPTER 15

Forever Love, Forever Life

THUS SAYS THE LORD, YOUR REDEEMER,
AND HE WHO FORMED YOU FROM THE WOMB:
"I AM THE LORD, WHO MAKES ALL THINGS."
Isaiah 44:24

Faith begins...

For me, faith begins with the realization that a supreme
intelligence brought the universe into being and created man.
It is not difficult for me to have this faith, for an orderly,
intelligent universe testifies to the greatest statement ever
uttered: 'In the beginning, God...'
*Arthur Compton, awarded the 1927 Nobel Prize in Physics for his
discovery of the transfer of energy from electromagnetic radiation
to a particle, known as the Compton effect.*

When confronted with the marvels of life and the universe,
one must ask why the only possible answers are religious. ... I
find a need for God in the universe and in my own life.
*Arthur L. Schawlow, shared the 1981 Nobel Prize in Physics
for the development of laser spectroscopy.*

I only trace the lines that flow from God.
*Albert Einstein, awarded the 1921 Nobel Prize in Physics for his work
in theoretical physics, especially the law of photoelectric effect.* ∎

My avocado tree

NOW CHRIST IS RISEN FROM THE DEAD.
1 Corinthians 15:20

I have various herbs growing on my kitchen windowsill, and decided to use the little remaining space to try to grow an avocado plant. I stuck four toothpicks into the middle section of the seed so it could rest half-submerged on the mouth of a small jar filled with water—and waited.

Weeks went by, and there was no sign of life. By all appearances, it could have been a stone rather than a seed! When a month had gone by I considered giving up. Perhaps there was no life in this dull brown seed.

Then a tiny crack appeared at its base. I thought at this point that the seed might simply be drying out, but I was willing to wait a little longer. I changed the water, and a few more weeks passed. Finally a tiny root emerged from the crack. Then another crack appeared, this time at the top of the seed. Slowly but surely a small shoot peeked out hopefully.

Transplanted to a pot of soil, the seed that had appeared lifeless is now growing into a small but healthy plant. Tender green leaves sprout day by day, each growing to several times the size of the seed. This baby tree is proof that there was life inside the seed, despite outward appearances.

When Easter approaches, I am reminded of my avocado-growing experience. How hopeless Jesus' followers must have felt when they saw Him die on the cross! They watched His lifeless body be carried off and sealed in a stone-cold tomb. They must have felt as though their hopes and dreams were being buried too. I can picture them now, forlorn and seemingly forsaken. Yet hope was not dead! Three days later Jesus would rise triumphant, the victor over death and the grave.

The miracle of Jesus' resurrection is of course a far greater miracle than my little avocado plant, but what an example that plant is. Even when the outlook seems hopeless, wait on the Lord, and He will work miracles—new life, new hope, new beginnings!

Abi May ∎

Resurrection—how it works

Someone will say, "How are the dead raised up? And with what body do they come?"

What you sow is not made alive unless it dies. And what you sow, you do not sow that body that shall be, but mere grain—perhaps wheat or some other grain. But God gives it a body as He pleases, and to each seed its own body.

So also is the resurrection of the dead. The body is sown in corruption, it is raised in incorruption. It is sown in dishonor, it is raised in glory. It is sown in weakness, it is raised in power. It is sown a natural body, it is raised a spiritual body. There is a natural body, and there is a spiritual body.

Now this I say, brethren, that flesh and blood cannot inherit the kingdom of God; nor does corruption inherit incorruption. Behold, I tell you a mystery: We shall not all sleep, but we shall all be changed—in a moment, in the twinkling of an eye, at the last trumpet. For the trumpet will sound, and the dead will be raised incorruptible, and we shall be changed. For this corruptible must put

on incorruption, and this mortal must put on immortality. So when this corruptible has put on incorruption, and this mortal has put on immortality, then shall be brought to pass the saying that is written: "Death is swallowed up in victory." "O Death, where is your sting? O Hades, where is your victory?"

Thanks be to God, who gives us the victory through our Lord Jesus Christ.

1 Corinthians 15:35–38,42–44,50–55,57

Science has found that nothing can disappear without a trace. Nature does not know extinction. All it knows is transformation. If God applies the fundamental principle to the most minute and insignificant parts of the universe, doesn't it make sense to assume that He applies it to the masterpiece of His creation—the human soul? I think it does.

Wernher von Braun, rocket scientist and space architect ∎

The ant and the grasshopper

At a primary school, during their weekly class on morals, a group of first-grade students were asked to finish the story of the hard-working ant and the lazy grasshopper in the way they thought would be best.

Most of us know this story—one of Aesop's fables—of how the Grasshopper wasted the summer months playing his fiddle while the Ant labored hard storing food for the winter. When cold finally came, the industrious Ant and his friends were all safely tucked away with all that they would need, while the Grasshopper was left to search for food and found himself dying of hunger.

The six-year-olds were asked to draw a picture of and rewrite the ending of the story in any way they would like, but it needed to involve the Grasshopper asking the Ant for help. About half of the first-graders took the general view that since the Grasshopper was undeserving, the Ant refused to help him. The other half changed the end to say that the Ant told the Grasshopper to learn his lesson, and then he gave the Grasshopper half of what he had.

Then a little boy stood up and gave this version of the tale: After the Grasshopper came to the Ant and begged for food, the Ant unhesitatingly gave all the food he had. Not half or most, but everything. The boy was not finished, however, and cheerfully continued, "The Ant didn't have any food left, so he died. But then the Grasshopper was so sad that the Ant had died that he told everyone what the Ant had done to save his life. And the Grasshopper became a good Grasshopper."

Two things came to mind when this story was related to me. First, it reminded me what giving meant to Jesus. He didn't go halfway for us, and He didn't say we were "undeserving," but He gave His all so that we could learn to "be good." It was only through Him totally sacrificing His life that we were able to receive the gift of eternal life. It was just the way the Ant died for the Grasshopper in the six-year-old's retelling of the classic tale. And for us it should also not end there. In gratitude, we should follow His example and give our all to tell of the wonderful thing He did for us.

Second, I learned what it means to give your all. It is not true giving unless it hurts, but when you do truly give, it will be multiplied many times over. "Unless a grain of wheat falls into the ground and dies, it remains alone." But it doesn't end there. Here is the bittersweet promise that makes it all worthwhile: "But if it dies, it produces much grain."[1]

Retold by Tomoko Matsuoka ∎

[1] John 12:24

When Earth's last picture
is painted

When Earth's last picture is painted
and the tubes are twisted and dried,
When the oldest colors have faded,
and the youngest critic has died,
We shall rest, and, faith, we shall need it—
lie down for an eon or two,
Till the Master of All Good Workmen
shall put us to work anew!

And those that were good shall be happy:
they shall sit in a golden chair;
They shall splash at a ten-league canvas
with brushes of comets' hair.
They shall find real saints to draw from—
Magdalene, Peter, and Paul;
They shall work for an age at a sitting
and never be tired at all!

And only The Master shall praise us,
and only The Master shall blame;
And no one shall work for money,
and no one shall work for fame;
But each for the joy of the working,
and each, in his separate star,
Shall draw the Thing as he sees It
for the God of Things as They Are!
Rudyard Kipling ∎

Not long before his death in 1990, the British journalist Malcolm Muggeridge wrote, "I see my ancient carcass, prone between the sheets, stained and worn like a scrap of paper dropped in the gutter and, hovering over it, myself, like a butterfly released from its chrysalis stage and ready to fly away. Are caterpillars told of their impending resurrection?—How in dying they will be transformed from poor earth-crawlers into creatures of the air, with exquisitely painted wings? If told, do they believe it? I imagine the wise old caterpillars shaking their heads—no, it can't be; it's a fantasy."

And so it is with us. We've been told in the Bible what happens—or at least what can happen—to our souls, the "real us," when we come to the end of this life and shed our earthly bodies. And like those caterpillars, we have been given the choice to believe it or not.

That's the crunch, the pivotal point, the one condition on which the door to eternal life in heaven hinges—belief. "I am the resurrection and the life," Jesus said. "He who believes in Me, though he may die, he shall live."[1]

The miracle of Easter is that because Jesus didn't remain in the grave, we don't have to either. We don't have to suffer eternal separation from God as the payment for our sins. After taking that punishment for us, Jesus rose to life again. And because He lives, we can live also.[2] All it takes is belief in Jesus' redeeming sacrifice.

If you believe, you're good to go! And you just might be surprised at how little faith it takes. If all you can muster is the prayer of one desperate man in the Bible, "Lord, help my unbelief,"[3] you're opening your mind and heart to Jesus and giving Him a chance to prove Himself, and He will.

Keith Phillips ■

[1] John 11:25

[2] John 14:19

[3] Mark 9:24

Try me

WE KNOW THAT THE SON OF GOD HAS COME AND HAS GIVEN US AN
UNDERSTANDING, THAT WE MAY KNOW HIM WHO IS TRUE; AND WE
ARE IN HIM WHO IS TRUE, IN HIS SON JESUS CHRIST. THIS IS THE
TRUE GOD AND ETERNAL LIFE.

1 John 5:20

If you don't know Me yet, then I have a proposal for you: Rather
than trying to figure Me out, why not give Me a chance to show
you the truth? I am not just talking about right and wrong, or good
advice, but supernatural truth. All that I am cannot be comprehended
by the mind. You have to seek and understand with your heart. Why
not see for yourself if I'm real and "the way, the truth, and the life" as
I told My first disciples?[1] Why not put Me to the test? Accept My love
and presence into your life, and then see what I can do for you.

I can be your closest friend and confidant. I can help you when
things go wrong and you need support. I can give happiness in
place of grief, and I can bring beauty out of the ashes of failures and
mistakes. Once you ask Me into your life, I will never leave you.
That's a solemn pledge! I will always love and care for you in spite of
everything, including your own faults and failings.

Once you connect with Me personally, then as you delve into what
I have revealed in the Bible—and particularly in the Gospels—you
will discover pure and life-giving truths within My Word. There's a
personal message from Me to you within that book.

All you need to do to start to receive all that I have to offer is open
your heart and invite Me in.

A message from Jesus received in prayer ■

[1] John 14:6

Afterword

Behold, I stand at the door and knock. If anyone hears My voice and opens the door, I will come in to him and dine with him, and he with Me.

Revelation 3:20

God's love is all-powerful, but He won't force it on you. Instead, He sends His Son, Jesus, to knock at the door of your heart and then wait for you to open the door and invite Him in.

Jesus wants to give you eternal life and become a very real part of your life here and now, but He can't do either unless you want Him to. He stands meekly and patiently at your heart's door—perhaps He has been standing there for years—waiting for you to hear Him knocking and open. He wants to be your Savior and will come in as soon as you ask Him to, but He has left that choice up to you.

Will you accept Jesus Christ as your personal Savior? If you haven't already or if you're not sure that you're saved, you can make sure right now by sincerely praying this prayer:

Jesus, please forgive me for all my sins. I believe that You died for me. I open the door to my heart and I invite You into my life. Please fill me with Your love, help me get to know You, and guide me in the way of truth. Amen.

If you prayed that prayer and meant it, Jesus has already come in. You have eternal life and have just embarked on this life's greatest adventure—experiencing God's love in Jesus and growing in His ways and wisdom.

He lives! He lives!
Christ Jesus lives today!
He walks with me,
And talks with me,
Along life's narrow way.

He lives! He lives!
Salvation to impart.
You ask me how I know He lives,
He lives within my heart!
Alfred H. Ackley

From Jesus with love

I love you as if you were the only one. My love is reaching out to you right now. My love, My forgiveness, and My mercy are all right there, just for you, if you will only receive them.

I love you just the way you are. I am not stacking up all your faults and failures and mistakes to hold against you. I see only the good, and I see possibilities that others do not see.

I see your every tear. I hear your every cry. I feel your every frustration, your every worry, your every burden, your every desire. I know everything about you—all your wants, all your lacks. I see straight through to your heart of hearts and all that is in it, and I deeply love you. I am right there by your side, and I will never, ever forsake you.

I love you, just you, and here I patiently wait—for you! Won't you please come running into My arms, where we can live and love and revel in this love forever, eternally, immortally, without end? I'm yours.

A message from Jesus received in prayer ■

OTHER TITLES IN THIS SERIES